Cook, Pray, Eat Kosher

Cook, Pray, Eat Kosher
The Essential Kosher Cookbook for the Jewish Soul

Mia Adler Ozair

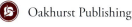 Oakhurst Publishing

 Feldheim Publishers

Copyright © 2015 by Mia Adler Ozair

All rights reserved. This book or any portion thereof may not be reproduced or used in any manner whatsoever without the express written permission of the publisher except for the use of brief quotations in a book review. No part of this publication may be stored in a retrieval system, or transmitted in any form or by any means, electronic, mechanical, photocopying, recording, scanning, or otherwise without prior written consent of the Publisher. THE RIGHTS OF THE COPYRIGHT HOLDER WILL BE STRICTLY ENFORCED.

PRINTED IN THE UNITED STATES OF AMERICA

First Printing, 2015

ISBN 978-0-9906014-1-8

Oakhurst Publishing Los Angeles, CA
Distribution by Feldheim Publishers

Book Design: Rafael van Winkel
Project Editors: Brenda Goldstein, Tanya Wlodarczyk
Photo Credits: Rachel Kessler, Mia Adler Ozair, Daniel Ricardo

Limit of Liability/Disclaimer: While the author and publisher have used their best efforts in preparing this book as accurately and completely as possible, they make no representations or warranties with respect to accuracy or completeness of the contents of this book and shall not be held liable for any loss or inaccuracy. The advice and strategies contained herein may not be suitable for your situation. Please consult with a professional where appropriate.

Ordering Information/Fundraising Projects: Special discounts are available on quantity purchases by corporations, associations, and others. For details on quantity sales or to organize a speaking/book signing or fundraising event, contact at **office@miaadlerozair.com**.

www.miaadlerozair.com

Dedications

Dedicated to our favorite *Neshamot*:

✣ Tamara
✣ Daniella
✣ Yosef
✣ Yael
✣ Eitan
✣ David
✣ Iyla
✣ Tsilah
and
✣ Yonatan

and to some of our favorite *tzadikim, z'l*:

✣ Rabbi Yonatan Ben Uziel
✣ Rabbi Yosef Chaim ("*Ben Ish Chai*")
✣ Rabbi Isaac Luria ("The *Ari*")
✣ Rabbi Akiva
✣ The Rebbe Schneerson
✣ Hoshea Ben Be'Eri
✣ Rabbi Amram Ben Diawan
✣ Rabbi Levi Yitzchak of Berditchev

Oma and Opa

To my Oma and Opa

I dedicate this book to you,
my beautiful
Oma and Opa
Thank you for filling my
childhood with joy

Oma,
you were a shining example in the kitchen,
and some of my greatest memories are of
cooking and baking at your side.

Opa,
you have taught me to only accept the best,
and to always give my best. It was my greatest joy as a child to visit you at work
and to watch you with all those who admired you so.
You were simply the best.

I miss you both.

With love,
Mia

Contents

Acknowledgements **15**
Foreword **17**
Introduction **19**
Food and the *Neshama* **23**
Food and *Mussar* **25**
Keys to *Kashrut* and this Cookbook **27**
Opposites Attract **31**

The Sacred *Challah* **34**
The *Mitzvah* of *Challah* 37
Challah by Hand (P) 39
Challah by Food Processor (P) 41
Michal's Water *Challah* (P) 43
Other *Challah* Tips 45
Soft Pretzels (P) 46
Basic Pizza Dough (P) 46

Meat **48**
Cocktail Hotdogs (KP, M) 50
Chopped Liver (KP, M) 50
Simple Brisket (KP, M) 53
Shabbat Cholent, (*Hamin*) (M) 54
Honey Brisket (KP, M) 55
Beauty Roast (KP, M) 56
Sweet and Sour Meatballs (KP, M) 57
Ma Catapan's Meatloaf (M) 58
Chili Con Carne (M) 58
Iraqi Meatballs with Green Peas (M) 61
Oma's Meat Spaghetti Sauce (KP, M) 62

Oma's Rouladen (M) 65
Five-Star Minute Steak (KP, M) 67
Bambia (KP, M) 68
Brisket and Onions (KP, M) 70
Mia's Mustard Braised Brisket (KP, M) 71
Lauren's Sloppy Joes (KP, M) 73
Boeuf Bourguignon (M) 75

Poultry 78
Chicken Wings Mandarin (M) 80
Chicken with 40 Cloves Garlic (KP, M) 81
Stir Fry Chicken (KP, M) 83
Saphi's Chicken (KP, M) 84
Honey Mustard Chicken (KP, M) 84
Whole Chicken Baked on Kosher Salt (KP, M) 86
Chicken Sepharadi (KP, M) 87
Tabit (Sepharadi Chicken and Rice) (M) 88

Fish 90
Simple Salmon (KP, P) 93
Gefilte Fish (KP, P) 94
Moroccan Fish (KP, P) 97
Tuna Salad (P) 98
Salmon Salad (P) 98

Vegetables 100
Oma's Red Cabbage (KP, M) 102
Baked Sweet Potatoes (KP, P) 104
Scalloped Corn Casserole (P, D) 105
Sweet Potato Casserole (D, P, KP) 107
Roasted Garlic (KP, P) 108
Roasted Red Potatoes (KP, P) 108
Glazed Carrots (P, KP) 111
Baked Onions (D, P, KP) 111

Soups **112**
French Onion Soup (D, P, KP) 114
Asian Shiitake Mushroom Soup (M, P) 116
Leek, Carrot and Potato Soup (D, M, P, KP) 117
Vegetable Soup (D, P, KP) 119
Easy *Matzo* Ball Soup (M, P, KP) 120
Chicken Soup to Heal Your Soul (M, KP) 122

Salads & Dips **124**
Terrific Oriental Salad (P) 126
Three-Bean Salad (P) 127
Sweet and Sour Cucumbers (KP, P) 127
Simple Egg Salad (KP, P) 129
Spicy Egg Salad (KP, P) 129
Matbucha (KP, P) 130
Simple Corn Salad (P) 130
Summer Potato Salad (KP, P) 131
Simple Guacamole (KP, P) 132
Kamoosh (KP, P, D) 132
Hummus (P) 135
Artichoke Spread (D, KP) 135

Pizza & Pasta **136**
Meatless Lasagna (D) 138
Traditional Thin-Crust Pizza (D) 141
Baked Noodles and Rice (D, M, P) 143
Orange Noodle Pudding (D) 144

Desserts **146**
Cookie Cheesecake (D) 148
Oma's Crescent Moon Cookies (D) 151
The Best Pareve Brownies (P) 152
Luscious Lemon Squares (P) 155
Baklava (D, P) 156
Toffee Squares (P) 158

Sesame Halava (P) 159
Adler Family Cheesecake (D) 161
Turtle Bars (D, P) 162
Banana Cake (P) 163
Pumpkin Bread (P) 163
Apple Crisp (D, P) 164
Chocolate Covered Dates (P) 166
Taffy Apples (KP, P) 167
Pareve Ice Cream (KP, P) 167
Chocolate Peanut Butter Diamonds (D, P) 168

Shabbat & Chaggim **170**
   A Word About This Section 173

Lichvod Shabbat Kodesh **175**
The Month of *Tishrei* **177**
Rosh Hashanah **178**
Yom Kippur **181**
Sukkot **183**

Chanukah **185**
   Potato Latkes (P) 185
   Chanukah Sufganiyot (D, P) 186

Tu B'Shvat **189**

Purim **190**
   Hamantaschen (P) 190

Pesach **195**
Kashrut and *Pesach* 197
Ashkenazi-Style *Charoset* (KP, P) 198
Sepharadi-Style *Charoset* (KP, P) 198
Popover Rolls (KP, P) 199
Almond Chicken (KP, M) 199

Broccoli-Spinach Casserole (KP, P, M) 201
Apple *Matzo* Kugel (KP, P) 201
Apple, Blueberry, and Cherry Cobbler (KP, P) 202
Pesach Fudgies (KP, P) 203
Passover Brownies (KP, P) 203

Shavuot **204**
Cheese Bourekas (D) 206
Mushroom and Cheese Blintzes (D) 206

Yahrzeit/Hilulah **209**

Glossary of Terms **210**
About the Author **213**
Resources **214**
Index **215**

Contents ❋ 13

Acknowledgements

With special thanks to:

My mom, who fields my calls at all hours of the day to guide me in the kitchen and answer my questions, about cooking and life, with love and patience.

Our moms and grandmothers, who have nurtured us with their love and inspired us with their cooking through the generations.

Our dads and grandfathers, who work hard, provide for their families, and every now and then dabble in the kitchen.

Rabbi David Toledano, endless thank yous.

Rafael van Winkel for his amazing talent, dedication, and patience in working with me to graphically design and lay out this book, without him this book would still be scattered pages in a box.

Brenda Goldstein & Tanya Wlodarczyk, my project editors, whose time and talent polished these pages.

Suzanne Brandt and Eli Hollander at Feldheim Publishing for believing in the power of this book and working with me to create a beautiful finished product.

Lauren Groveman, my cooking muse, friend, and inspiration to find my inner gourmet.

Laura Frankel, who has been incredibly supportive, kind, and available to me through my process with this book.

All of the amazing "gourmets" whose recipes are found within these pages.

Lena Kushnir and Susan Raihoffer, two women who never stop believing in me.

The many angels who come in many forms and in many ways to give guidance, support, love, and encouragement.

and, of course,
My husband. May HaShem bless you with a long, healthy, and prosperous life, and may we have the privilege of sharing it together.

Foreword

Countless hours have been spent on the pages you're about to indulge in, and indulge you will. The warmth, care, and delicious love for family, food, and tradition can be felt on every page.

Mia weaves family, food, culture and halacha together in a gentle, loving way. She carefully narrates holiday menus, cook's tips, and kashrut with knowledge and description that will have newbies and experienced kosher home cooks learning and appreciating the holidays.

Like peeking into a family's photo albums, Mia has gathered anecdotes, recipes, and tips from her family's history and current blend of Ashkenazi and Sephardi lives. I think every cook who loves food and history will appreciate this gathering of memories.

I have the pleasure of having known Mia since she was a child. Her father, Larry, was the President of our synagogue. I remember an annual Kol Nidre appeal (Eve of Yom Kippur) when he stood up in front of the congregation and said "**The family that prays together stays together.**" I would further that with Mia's book: the family that **eats, prays, and cooks kosher together, stays together!**

Mia's family recipes are delicious, span generations, and will surely become treasured family recipes in your own kitchen.

Whether you are setting up a kosher kitchen or looking for new recipe ideas to add to your repertoire, **Cook, Pray, Eat Kosher** is a heartwarming and tasty read.

Executive Chef Laura Frankel
Author ***Jewish Cooking For All Seasons*** and
Jewish Slow Cooker Recipes
(John Wiley and Sons)

Introduction

If anyone would have told me a few years back that I would be putting together my own cookbook I would have laughed. Not because I'm a horrible cook or don't like cooking, but rather because I've never considered myself to be anything special in the kitchen and I'm also not a particularly picky eater. As long as the food is healthy and has some flavor, I'm good. I knew how to make the basics and didn't venture much into unknown cooking or baking territory. In short, I kept it safe in the kitchen. This was all good and fine and working well for me. My kids ate my food and seemed to enjoy it with no major complaints. We had our favorite dishes that were primarily those of my mom's recipes (which are, of course, still some of our favorites.) However, things took a sharp turn when into my life strolled Mr. Tall, Dark, and Handsome Israeli-Iraqi Guy. You see, he threw me off at first. On our first date he took me to the legendary Pat's Steak House in the Pico/Robertson neighborhood here in L.A. It doesn't get more "meat and potatoes" than Pat's. Translation: Ashkenazi kosher cuisine at its finest! Silly me, I thought I had it made: an Israeli-Iraqi who eats Ashkenazi style—the exact type of foods I know how to make. Right? WRONG! Well, not entirely wrong. He does love a good steak, but hidden beneath that palate lies a traditional Middle-Eastern Sephardic man who loves his spice and his traditional Sephardic dishes. Fortunately, he was quite good in the kitchen and was able to teach me a thing or two about how to bridge our cooking cultural differences. The result? A home filled with a variety of amazing foods from different lineages, all of it made with love and care.

Just like our paths in cooking blended from differing backgrounds, our viewpoints and practice of Judaism was also differing for my husband and me. I have personally studied various aspects of Judaic text and spiritual study for over two decades having first been more deeply interested in these matters at the age of 16. I started my path in the Conservative Movement and over the course of my life have settled in the Orthodox movement. My husband was a mostly secular Jew growing up in Israel and starting his Orthodox lifestyle in his mid-twenties. Like most, his practice took twists and turns as he made his way through life and today we share a traditional Orthodox Jewish lifestyle with our combination of kids. I call my husband, "*Rebbe Shaul*", Mr. Halacha (making reference to his vast knowledge of and adherence to Jewish law), and he calls me his *Neshama*, his soul, which is an accurate representation of my underlying paradigm about the spiritual side of life and how all of

that intersects with the "rules and regulations" so-to-speak. In essence, our cooking, and our personal views about Judaism and life, come from different vantage points ultimately creating a rich, tasty, and enriching blend of life together.

As you read this cookbook, in addition to great recipes you will also find golden nuggets of wisdom based deeply in Torah and Jewish texts. I thank my *Talmid Hacham* (Torah scholar) husband for helping me integrate these meaningful threads into the book. It is my hope that our combined wisdom illuminates some new elements for the Jewish kitchen that will enrich your own.

Here is where it all begins: Our connection to food is deep and complex, and a necessity to survival in the Human Experience. The interactive dynamics between food, body, and soul teach us that, through food, *HaShem* (G-d) has provided us with a means for not only sustaining us physically, but spiritually, as well. According to *Kabbalah*, every piece of food–including the smallest piece of grain–holds a spark of Light just waiting to be released. When we participate in the act of eating, it is the combination of our blessings on the food, along with the chewing and digesting of that food, that then releases that Light to return to *HaShem* and to provide us–both physically and spiritually–with sustenance and nourishment. It is, quite simply, an awesome process.

Given that so much of our lives revolves around food, (selecting, purchasing, preparing, eating, and cleaning up after) and given that food plays such an integral role in the life of a Jewish family (what we can eat, how and when we can eat it, plus the connection between food and holidays or life-cycle events of all kinds), it would seem that developing a healthy relationship with food can only benefit us on all levels.

In creating this cookbook, my intention is to not only equip you with some great recipes, but hopefully to inspire you to see how your relationship with food can elevate you and your family. There are so many *halachot* (Jewish laws) about "how" and "what" when it comes to food–all of which are important. However, the one thing that we *must* do, regardless of our religious background, is to always strive to find ways to grow spiritually, to challenge ourselves, and to find the delicate balance one must have in order to create a healthy connection with food and with life.

Our relationship with food is a direct reflection of our relationship with *HaShem*. Do we rush? Do we give thanks? Do we eat too much? Too little? Do we appreciate the food, its source, and its service to us? Do we give to others who might have less or not have at all?

As you read through the pages of this cookbook, I hope you find some new sparks, something that resonates and pushes you to try new things. Taste new foods, explore new methods of cooking, take upon yourself a new *mitzvah* that perhaps you haven't had the vessel for in the past. Most important, share your discoveries with others and be an inspiration for others through your own process.

I used to be so intimidated by the demands of being *shomer Shabbat* (keeping the Sabbath) and preparing food for *Shabbat* and *chaggim* (holidays). I felt nervous about timing everything and knew very little about finding my way around a kitchen. The truth is (*and don't tell him this!*) my husband, Shaul, was without question a better cook than I was at the time that we got married. However, with time, guidance from some amazing people and practice, merging an observant Jewish lifestyle with fancy footwork in the kitchen is now second nature to me–and it can be for you, as well. If, in any way, this book brings you closer to *HaShem* and closer to those around you, then it will have been a great success.

Wishing you all the best as you discover, or refine, your inner gourmet! May your table always be overflowing with beautiful food and meaningful guests, and may all who sit there be blessed with great health, joy, abundance, and *bitachon* (trust) in *HaShem*.

    With Love,
    Mia Adler Ozair
    Los Angeles, CA.
    Sivan *5775*
    June 2015

10 percent of all net proceeds from this book goes to support Jewish education.
To use this book as a fundraiser, please contact Mia.

Food and the Neshama

The Ultimate Connection
Cooking for someone is one of the most spiritual and intimate acts of creation and sharing. *In what other circumstance does something you create actually become a part of another person?* Think about it: the food we eat breaks down into all its important components, nutrients flowing freely through the body actually being absorbed by the cells in order to sustain us. Although all people eat in order to survive, for the Jewish person specifically, eating is meant to be a way to elevate our connection with G-d.

Ruach*, *Nefesh*, and *Neshama
Ruach is the most basic level of the soul that is most closely connected with the physical body. It is this level of the soul that sustains our body's systems–our heart beating, our lungs breathing, etc. *Nefesh* is the mid-level of the soul and acts as the "go-between" for the higher and lower levels of the soul. The *Neshama* is one of the highest levels of the soul and is the part of the soul that connects us with G-d–it is the part of G-d that exists within us and it is this same part that enables us to elevate our consciousness through purposeful endeavors such as study of *Torah*, doing *Mitzvot* (commandments and good deeds) or giving *Tzedaka* (charity). (There do exist two other, higher levels to the Jewish soul, typically received only by *Tzaddikim*, righteous people.)

Kashrut* and the *Neshama
The Jewish *Neshama* has special requirements in order for it to make the strongest connections with G-d. Foremost, the Jewish *Neshama* requires that the Jewish body follow the laws of *kashrut* and only eat those foods that are permissible. Why, in this day and age, would *kashrut* still be required? Put simply, the body is our vessel. It is our own personal temple for our *Neshama*. In order for the *Neshama* to be able to engage fully, the Jewish body must be kept in a certain manner and kosher food is what maintains this balance for the Jewish *Neshama*. The spiritual laws of *kashrut* fill volumes of books. However, every Jewish text that exists, from *Gemara* and *Halacha* to *Zohar* and *Kabbalah*, states clearly that one of the first and most powerful steps to connecting with *HaShem* is through keeping the laws of *kashrut*.

Blessings and the *Neshama*
In addition to the laws of *kashrut*, the *Neshama* also requries that we say *brachot*, blessings, before and after we eat. The most common reason given for this is to say thank you to *HaShem* for the food given to us. Although nice, the meanings behind the blessings are so much deeper and more meaningful than simply giving thanks. Within every single grain of food, piece of fruit, or drop of water, there exists a spark of Light, a piece of *HaShem*, waiting to be released. The Jewish *Neshama* is given the power to elevate and release these sparks of Light by saying the appropriate blessings both before and after we eat. Can you imagine? Suddenly, eating is no longer something we do because we are hungry, but rather something we do for the sake of strengthening our connection to G-d. Suddenly, it becomes more clear why Jewish holidays and celebrations always seem to incorporate meals with special blessings for that holiday or particular event or meal. We are given a powerful gift in this regard and one worth exploring. The *brachot* for any number of foods can be found in most *siddurim*, prayer books, or can be found online.

Your role and responsibility as creator
Given that our universe is one vast metaphysical system, with everything being made up of various energies, it is important to know that you, chef extraordinaire, leave your mark on whatever food you prepare. Your thoughts, feelings, and energies go into your food much the same as the actual food, once eaten, becomes a part of the body. I have developed my own personal ritual of prayer that I say before I prepare food for anyone, especially *challot* for *Shabbat* and *chaggim*. I often begin with the powerful prayer, *Ana B'Koach*, found in most prayer books or online. I then go on to say something like this: "*HaShem*, please bless whoever eats this food with excellent health, much happiness, abundant wealth, and much love. May he/she be inspired to do *mitzvot* and to bring peace to the world." If you like this idea, feel free to borrow from my prayer or to create your own. Either way, simply having a consciousness of what it means to create food for someone can instantly elevate your connection with *HaShem,* as well as your connection with those lucky ones who get to enjoy your food.

Food and Mussar

How to use the act of eating to elevate your soul

Mussar is the Jewish spiritual practice of self-development that involves internally refining character traits in order to better connect with G-d and to become the best version of one's self. It is a deep and meaningful practice to fill volumes of books, but for our purposes, I'd like to entertain the idea of connecting basic concepts of *Mussar* with our divine and essential relationship with food.

Mussar involves the internal investigation of various traits, or *middot*, that provides us with lenses for focus of self-correction. I've selected a few of these *middot* for consideration. Instead of providing answers, I've merely provided "food for thought" in the form of questions relating to the specific *middah*. The idea is to develop and/or enhance these traits in our lives, which, in turn, lead to greater awareness and consciousness.

Food for Thought:
When considering your personal relationship with G-d and his creation of the human necessity to eat:

The *middah* of Gratitude (*Hakarat Ha'Tov*):
How do I show thanks for the food that my family and I eat each day? Why do I (or don't I)? What energy and effort goes into the growing and making of the food that sits in front of me to consume? How deep is my understanding of sustenance?

The *middah* of Order (*Seder*):
There are three "*seders*" we participate in each year during *Pesach*, *Rosh Hashana*, and *Tu' B'shvat*. What is the connection between these mystical events and this *middah* of "order?" Why are we given these opportunities to eat certain foods in certain ways with certain blessings at certain times? How do the concepts of *kashrut* and the *middah* of order intersect to impact body and soul?

The *middah* of Moderation (*Shevil Ha'Zahov*):
The body is a delicate system of checks and balances and this system is greatly influenced by the foods we eat. How does the *middah* of moderation apply to our relationship with food? Why do the body and soul need moderation and balance to thrive?

The *middah* of Generosity (*Nedivut*):
How often am I concerned with and take action for those who have little or no food? What of those who have food, but no one with whom to enjoy it?

Keys to Kashrut and This Cookbook

The laws of *kashrut* (keeping kosher), especially regarding the preparation and cooking of foods for *Shabbat* and *chaggim*, are detailed. Below you will find some general, overarching guidelines for *kashrut* that are a great place to start. *It is always best to consult your Rabbi or reputable books or texts for specific issues or for learning in greater detail.* Each recipe in this book is identified as meat (M), dairy (D), and/or *pareve* (P). If the recipe can be made kosher for Passover it also has a (KP) listing.

General things to remember about *kashrut*:

❖ Foods that are either meat (M) or dairy (D) are never prepared, cooked, served, or consumed together.
❖ Foods that are *pareve* (P) are considered "neutral" and can generally be prepared, cooked, served, or consumed together with either meat or dairy foods at any given meal. There are exceptions to this for various customs in various communities. For example, various branches of Sepharadi Jews do not eat cheese (D) with fish (P), where some Ashkenazi Jews will eat those items together. It is best to consult your Rabbi for specifics about your community's practices.
❖ All vegetables must be carefully washed and checked for any bugs.
❖ Food may never be cooked on *Shabbat*. All food must be cooked prior to *Shabbat* and can be warmed on a warming plate (*blech*). In memory of the Sassoon Family tragedy please be certain your *blech* is safe and that your home is well equipped with proper smoke and fire detectors. *Zichronam l'vracha*, may their memory be for a blessing.

❖ Slow cooker pots are available and are useful for cooking foods over several hours such as *cholent*, *hamin*, or *tabit*. These pots start the cooking prior to *Shabbat* and continue into *Shabbat*, but the pot itself is not turned off until after *Shabbat*. Important note: when using a slow cooker, it is important to know that it is not permissible to add any seasonings or to even stir the food inside the pot, as this is considered "cooking" and will violate *Shabbat*, causing the food to be inedible.
❖ The inner crock must be removed prior to serving or a timer set to shut it off prior to serving.
❖ Cooking is permissible on *chaggim* through the "transferring of fire," meaning, if you have a large candle burning in your home that was lit before the start of the holiday, and you take fire from this candle to light the stove or oven (by-passing the electrical start) then you can cook over this fire. The fire may not be extinguished after use, so take caution to create a safe space around the source of fire.

And The Journey Begins...

Opposites Attract

Mishpachas *Adler* V' Mishpachas *Ozair*:
The Adler and Ozair Families' Cast of Characters

The German-American Ashkenazi Side

My mom, Angie Adler, was born in Germany to my Oma (Hilda), an outstanding cook, and my Opa (Karl), a professional five-star restaurant and country-club manager. Both my Oma and Opa taught me that, when it comes to food and food service, only the finest and absolute best will do. My mom, an outstanding cook in her own right, carried on the family tradition, making the holiday feasts to which everyone looks forward. My dad, Larry Adler, American-born and raised, didn't have much involvement in the kitchen until the 1990s, when he slowly took on the role of "Mom's Assistant." He sets one beautiful table and knows how to make excellent Passover popovers. I personally am a "meat and potatoes" kind of gal, spoiled by the gourmet foods of my European roots.

Ashkenazim: Jews of Central and Eastern Europe, or their descendants, distinguished from the Sepharadim chiefly by their liturgy, religious customs, and pronunciation of Hebrew.

The Iraqi-Israeli Sepharadi Side

My mother-in-law, Hana Manzur, descends from Morocco and is an incredible cook. When she comes to visit from Israel, we anxiously stand by her side in the kitchen, taking careful notes on how to make the traditional foods of the Middle East. My husband, Shaul, is also an excellent cook. He and I are often side-by-side in the kitchen, experimenting with new and exciting recipe ideas or attempting to perfect old favorites. Although his Iraqi-Israeli dad, Alfred Ozair, doesn't spend much time in the kitchen, he does bring me flowers every time he visits for a meal, and for this he gets bonus points and extra servings! Shaul is unquestionably a "the-spicier-the-better" kind of guy, holding true to the rich Middle Eastern flavors of Israel, Iraq, and Morocco.

Sepharadim: Jews of Spain and Portugal or their descendants, distinguished from the Ashkenazim and other Jewish communities chiefly by their liturgy, religious customs, and pronunciation of Hebrew. After expulsion from Spain and Portugal in 1492, they established communities in North Africa, the Balkans, Western Europe, and elsewhere.

The Sacred Challah

When HaShem *created the world, He took a part of the earth of* Eretz Yisrael *to create* Adam HaRishon *(The First Man), and called him* "Challato shel Olam", *the* Challah *of the World. When* HaShem *wished to create The First Woman, Eve, He took a part of* Adam HaRishon *and made* hafrashat challah *(separation of the* challah*) and this became Woman. When* Hashem *wishes to elevate something to a state of holiness, he makes a separation. This separated piece becomes the holiest of the whole. Such is the case of separating* Shabbat *from the weekdays, separating woman from man, and separating a piece of dough with each making of* challah. *That which has been separated is the holiest of holy in* HaShem's *creation.*

Gemarah Sanhedrin

My homemade challah *using the "Challah by Hand" recipe found on page 39*

The Mitzvah of Challah

Challah is the special bread made for *Shabbat* and *chaggim* that is used when reciting the "*HaMotzie*" blessing. The making of *challah* for *Shabbat* and *chaggim*, and the "taking of *challah*" to recite the special blessing of *Hafrashat Challah*, is one of three *mitzvot* commanded to Jewish women, the other two being to light the *Shabbat* candles and to practice the laws of *Taharat HaMishpacha* (or laws of *niddah*). In fact, Rabbi Menachem Mendel Schneerson, z'l, of the Chabad movement, explains that this *mitzvah* of *challah* is actually commanded to Jewish woman through the *Torah* itself.

The secrets of the *challah* are deep and numerous, connecting to both *halacha* and secrets of the *Zohar* and *Kabbalah*. We know that the taking of *challah* is connected to the Kabbalistic Tree of Life, *Etz HaChaim*, in the domain of *Binah*, translated as "understanding." A great number of books have been written on such matters that are too vast to cover here. However, it is important to know that when a woman does this *mitzvah,* she is connecting herself to an enormous cosmic energy that brings great Light to both her and her family.

In addition, the Light she brings into her home becomes a Light that supports all Jews around the world. The *mitzvah* of separating *challah* in the *Torah* is found in five verses in the portion of *Shlach Lecha* (Numbers 15:17-21). *Shlach Lecha* is the 37th portion of the *Torah*.

Although taking on the obligation of making *challah* can seem a huge undertaking in today's fast-paced lifestyle, with practice, this weekly ritual can become a sanctuary in time. I have found that preparing *challah* for *Shabbat* is an established time for me to get into the spiritual state of mind that *Shabbat* is meant for, and I also use this as a time to pray for my family and friends, or for anyone I know who will be partaking of the *challah* I am preparing.

How to Take *Challah* and Recite the Blessing:
✣ Prepare *challah* dough (recipes are on the following pages).
✣ According to *halacha*, in order to say the blessing, the recipe must produce a certain quantity of dough. Use the following as a guideline: 8-1/2 cups flour or less: no separation, no blessing; 10 to 12 cups flour: separation, no blessing; 14 cups flour or more: separation and blessing.

✤ *Challah* can be taken any time during the preparation of the dough, but should be prior to baking.

✤ At desired time (I usually do it after first rising of the dough), separate a golf-ball-size piece of *challah* while reciting the following prayer:

✤ "*Baruch Ata A-do-na-i El-o-hai-nu Me-lech Ha-Olam Asher Kiddishanu B'Mitzvotav Vitzivanu L'hafrish challah min ha-eesa (terumah).*" [Blessed are You, L-rd our G-d, King of the Universe, who has sanctified us with His commandments and commanded us to separate *challah* (*terumah*) (Sepharadim add the word "*terumah*" to the blessing, Ashkenazim omit this word).

✤ Take the piece of *challah* that has been removed, hold it up in your right hand and say, "*Ha'rei zo challah*" (This is *Challah*).

✤ Wrap separated dough in foil and burn over a gas burner or in the oven, or double wrap, and then dispose of it.

To learn more about the secrets of the Challah, *ask your Rabbi, visit Chabad.org, or search the subject on the Internet. All* challah *recipes in this book are* pareve.

Challah by Hand

**Makes: 4 large, 5 medium, or 6 small *challot*. This is enough dough to pull part of the *challah* and recite the blessing for the *mitzvah*
Source: Mia**

Ingredients

✤ 3 to 4 tablespoons active dry yeast
✤ 4-1/2 to 5 cups warm water
✤ 3 tablespoons salt
✤ 1/2 cup sugar
✤ 1-1/4 cups vegetable oil
✤ 4 eggs (or 7 eggs if choosing egg wash)
✤ 14 cups bread flour
✤ 2 tablespoons water for egg wash

This is truly a family heirloom recipe. There is nothing quite like homemade challah! *Best when warmed for 20 to 30 minutes prior to the meal. Just wrap in foil and allow to warm on* Shabbat *warmer.*

Recipe Instructions

✤ In a large bowl, sprinkle yeast over warm water; add pinch of sugar and let stand for five minutes to dissolve yeast.
✤ Stir in salt, sugar, oil, and four eggs.
✤ Gradually mix in flour, kneading to bring flour into mix.
✤ Once all flour is added, knead on floured surface for 10 minutes.
✤ Oil large bowl; place dough inside oiled bowl and then flip so that both sides are coatedwith oil.
✤ Cover with lightweight towel or cheese cloth and place in a quiet, nondrafty place. Allow to rise until double, approximately one and one-half to two hours.
✤ Punch down dough, and now is the best time to make *hafrasha*, say the blessing.
✤ Break into four, five, or six balls of dough, depending upon number of *challot* you are making.
✤ Knead each ball of dough for five minutes, then braid into either three- or six-strand *challah* and place on baking sheet lined with parchment paper or foil sprayed with olive oil cooking spray.
✤ Cover *challot* with lightweight towel or cheese cloth, and let rise another hour.
✤ Preheat oven to 375 degrees.
✤ At this point, if desired, beat remaining eggs with two tablespoons water for egg wash; brush a coating of beaten egg over *challot* and add sesame seeds or other topping.

Continued...

✤ Bake for 30 minutes. *Challah* should sound hollow when crust is gently knocked on bottom and should look golden brown (cooking times may vary depending upon oven).
✤ Remove from oven and move *challot* to cooling racks; allow to cool completely.
✤ If eating within the day, wrap tightly with plastic wrap and store at room temperature.
✤ If freezing, wrap with three layers of plastic wrap and then with foil, to prevent freezer burn.

Challah by Food Processor

Makes: 2 large *challot*
Source: Mom

Ingredients

✤ 1 packet dry yeast
✤ 3/4 cup warm water
✤ 1/4 cup sugar
✤ 1/4 cup oil
✤ 2 egg yolks separated from whites (save whites)
✤ 2-3/4 cups flour
✤ 3/4 teaspoon salt

This is not enough dough to separate challah *and make a blessing for* hafrashat challah.

Recipe Instructions

✤ Dissolve yeast in one quarter cup of warm water and a pinch of sugar. Stir, set aside to rest for 10 minutes.
✤ With steel blade in processor, add flour, sugar, and salt, and pulse together.
✤ Add yeast, pulse four times.
✤ Add two egg yolks, run machine, and slowly add half a cup of warm water and oil through funnel. Process for 60 to 90 seconds, adding a little flour if dough is sticky.
✤ Place in large oiled bowl (put one teaspoon of oil into bowl and spread around with paper towel), turn dough over so all sides are oiled. Poke dough three to four times with finger making deep holes, and then cover bowl with lightweight towel or cheese cloth.
✤ When dough has doubled in size (about one and a half to two hours) and holes are gone, punch down dough with fist.
✤ Take out of bowl and knead for one minute. Use flour on surface if sticking, then divide into three ropes, braid, and place on ungreased cookie sheet or cookie sheet lined with parchment paper.
✤ Allow to rise for one to one and a half hours and then preheat oven to 375 degrees (350 degrees if electric).

Continued...

- Mix egg whites with one teaspoon warm water and glaze *challah*. Add seeds if desired.
- Bake for 30 to 40 minutes until golden brown and hollow when knocked on the bottom.

Michal's Water Challah

Makes: 4 *challot*
Source: Michal Ben Menachem

Ingredients

✤ 14 cups flour
✤ 4 ounces active dry yeast
✤ 6-1/2 cups water
✤ 4 teaspoons salt
✤ 1/2 cup sugar
✤ 1/2 cup oil

For egg wash:
✤ 4 eggs, beaten well
✤ 1 tablespoon sugar
✤ sesame or poppy seeds (optional)

This recipe provides enough dough to make the blessing for hafrashat challah.

Recipe Instructions

To make dough:
✤ Add yeast to water and allow to sit for five to 10 minutes.
✤ Add oil, sugar, salt, and mix well.
✤ Slowly add cups of flour and mix/knead until all flour is taken into the mixture.
✤ Allow to rise for one hour.
✤ Punch down dough, separate into quantities of four *challot* and braid.
✤ Set aside on baking sheet to rise for an additional 30 minutes.

To bake dough:
✤ Preheat oven to 400 degrees.
✤ While oven is heating, make egg wash by mixing eggs and sugar together.
✤ Brush *challot* with egg wash and then sprinkle with desired seeds (optional).
✤ Place *challot* in oven at 400 degrees for 10 minutes, then reduce heat to 375 degrees and bake for 15 to 20 minutes until *challot* are golden brown and baked through.

Round Braided Challah

Other Challah Tips

Making Pull-Apart or Round *Challah*

Source: Mia

It is traditional on *Shabbat* and most *chaggim* to have braided *challot*. However, for certain chaggim, such as *Rosh Hashanah* and *Sukkot*, it is best to use round *challot* (related to the symbolisms of the cycles of life and other deeper connections).

There are two fun and easy ways to make round *challah*:

Method one: Using a spring pan, take a regular dough of *challah*, cut it into 10 sections and create 10 balls of dough. Place one ball in the center of the pan and nine surrounding. Bake as usual. This creates the favorite "pull-apart" *challah*.

Method two: Braid a *challah* as usual. Wrap one end to meet the other, slightly overlapping one end upon the other. Bake as usual.

Freezing Dough for Later Use

Method One:
Wrap dough tightly in three layers of plastic wrap. Thaw when needed for at least three hours. Knead, allow to rise for two hours. Shape and bake.

Method Two:
Allow dough to rise, shape into loaves, place in freezer until just hardened. Wrap in three layers of plastic wrap; freeze until needed. When thawing, remove plastic wrap, allow to thaw/rise for three hours, then bake.

Fun Doughs

Soft Pretzels

Makes: 12 to 15 large pretzels
Source: Kindergarten Teachers, Solomon Schechter Day School of Chicago

Ingredients

* 1 package active dry yeast (2-1/4 teaspoons)
* 1-1/2 cups warm water
* 1 teaspoon sugar
* 1 teaspoon salt
* 4 cups flour (use more if sticky)
* 1 egg, beaten
* Coarse kosher salt

Recipe Instructions

* Preheat oven to 425 degrees.
* Combine yeast with a little warm water and let stand five minutes.
* Add rest of water, sugar, salt, and flour.
* Press dough into shapes and place on greased cookie sheet.
* Brush with beaten egg and sprinkle with coarse salt.
* Bake 12 to 15 minutes.
* Best when eaten warm and most fun to make with kids!

Basic Pizza Dough

Makes: Two 12-inch crusts
Source: Irma Rombauer, Marion Rombauer Becker & Ethan Becker

Ingredients

* 1 package active dry yeast (2-1/4 teaspoons)
* 1-1/3 cups warm water
* 3-1/2 to 3-3/4 cups all purpose flour
* 2 tablespoons olive oil
* 1 tablespoon salt
* 1 tablespoon sugar (optional)

Recipe Instructions

* Allow yeast to proof (begin to bubble and churn) in warm water for five minutes, then add all ingredients and knead for about 10 minutes.
* Transfer to oil-coated bowl and allow to rise for one to one and a half hours.

For the full pizza recipe (D), see the Pizza & Pasta section.

Soft Pretzels

Meat

"There can be no joy without meat and wine!"

Gemarah Sanhedrin

Appetizers

Cocktail Hotdogs

Makes: 5 to 6 servings
Source: Mom

Ingredients

- 12 ounces bottled chili sauce
- 1/2 cup drained pineapple
- 1/2 cup jelly (strawberry or grape)
- 1-1/2 tablespoons brown sugar
- 1-1/2 tablespoons vinegar
- 3 dashes Tabasco® sauce
- 1/2 tablespoon Worcestershire® sauce
- 2 pounds cocktail hotdogs or regular hotdogs, cut diagonally

Recipe Instructions

- Heat all ingredients but hot dogs in saucepan, until blended.
- Add hotdogs and simmer for 10 minutes.
- Serve warm.

Chopped Liver

Makes: 6 to 8 servings
Source: Oma

Ingredients

Ratio: Two hard boiled eggs and one large onion to one pound of chicken livers.

- 3 pounds chicken livers, must be salted and broiled in order to be kosher
- 6 hard-boiled eggs
- 3 large onions
- *Pareve* margarine
- Salt and pepper, to taste

Recipe Instructions

- Using a wood skewer, grill livers over an open flame, until all blood has drained and meat is cooked through (this process is imperative for the livers to be kosher).
- Sauté onions in *pareve* margarine.
- Add thoroughly cooked livers to frying pan with onions and cook together a few more minutes.

Continued...

- Cut each egg into quarters and feed all three ingredients alternately into meat grinder.
- Mix ground ingredients together and add only salt and pepper to taste.
- Serve in bowl, or mold and shape.
- Can decorate with olives and serve with cocktail ryes and crackers (during *Pesach,* serve with *matzo* crackers).

Simple Brisket

Simple Brisket

Makes: 4 to 6 servings
Source: Liz Smith

Ingredients

* 5 pounds of "first cut" meat
* Allspice
* Garlic powder
* Salt
* Red wine
* Water

Optional:
* Potatoes
* Carrots
* Onions

Recipe Instructions

* Preheat oven to 350 degrees.
* Sprinkle each of the following thoroughly on both sides of meat: allspice, garlic powder, salt.
* Place in roasting pan and pour enough liquid to come up sides of meat at a ratio of one cup water to one cup wine.
* Cover and bake for at least two hours, averaging 20 minutes per pound of meat.
* Check every 30 minutes and add liquid in proper ratio as necessary.
* If desired, add potatoes, carrots and/or onions during last hour of cooking, but be sure to maintain adequate liquid during cooking.

I met Liz when I was pregnant with my second son a very long time ago. She and her family lived next door to us and little did I know she would become like a sister to me. The first time we were invited to Liz's home for Shabbat dinner she made this brisket and it was one of the best I'd ever had. Now, even though we live far apart and don't get to keep up as often as we'd like to, every time I make this brisket it's as if she is with me at my table.

Meat ❋ 53

Shabbat Cholent, (Hamin)

Makes: 8 to 10 servings
Source: Chaim

Ingredients

* 1 large can chick peas
* Dry beans of choice totaling 1 to 2 cups, depending on tastes
* 2 pounds cheek meat or beef shank, whole
* 3 small white potatoes, halved
* 3 small sweet potatoes, halved
* 3 to 4 eggs
* 2 bulbs garlic, whole, but peeled
* 1 large onion
* 1 to 2 tablespoons salt, pepper, cumin and tumeric (or to taste)
* 2 to 3 tablespoons chicken soup mix—dry powder
* 1/2 to 3/4 cup honey
* 5 to 6 cups water (or as needed)
* 1 cup rice

Use large electric slow-cooker for this dish.

Recipe Instructions

Layer as follows:

* Chick peas and all dry beans to cover bottom.
* Meat is put next on top of beans and chickpeas.
* Add potatoes whole and eggs in shell.
* Cut onion in half and add garlic bulbs.
* Add following to taste: salt, pepper, chicken soup mix, cumin, tumeric.
* Pour generous amount of honey over all ingredients and add water to within 1/2 inch from top of pot.
* For rice: in separate plastic bag, add one cup rice; two cups hot water; salt, pepper, cumin and tumeric to taste. Seal bag tightly with no air and place gently on top of cholent ingredients. Or, if preferred, sprinkle rice across top of other ingredients and add a touch of each spice sprinkled on top of rice (be sure there is plenty of water in pot to compensate for rice during cooking).
* Cover pot tightly; cook on high setting for three to four hours before *Shabbat*, then turn to medium setting just before *Shabbat* and leave for remainder of *Shabbat*.
* There are many *halachot* about cooking on *Shabbat*. It is important that once *Shabbat* begins, nothing is added to the pot and nothing is stirred while in the heating element. It is best if slow-cooker is on a timer set to shut off before serving, or cooking pot should be lifted out of heating element before serving. Please consult a Rabbi for more details.

Honey Brisket

Makes: 4 to 6 servings
Source: Adina Torchman

Ingredients

- 1 5-pound brisket
- 1 14-ounce jar ketchup
- 4 onions, sliced
- Paprika
- Garlic powder
- Pepper
- 2 bags carrots, cut up
- 3 pounds sweet potatoes, cut in quarters
- 1 12-ounce jar honey
- 2 pounds dried fruit (optional)
- 2 peels lemon

Recipe Instructions

- Preheat oven to 350 degrees.
- Place ketchup and onions in bottom of pan.
- Place brisket in pan on top of ketchup and onions.
- Season generously with paprika, garlic powder, and pepper.
- Cover and bake for one and a half hours.
- Uncover to add carrots, sweet potatoes, honey, dried fruit, lemon peel, more paprika, and water if dry.
- Bake covered for two hours or until done.
- Check liquid and add water and ketchup when necessary.

Beauty Roast

Makes: 6 servings
Source: Marcy Rotenberg

Ingredients

* 4-5 pounds Beauty Roast (eye of chuck or ribeye roast)
* Browning sauce of choice
* Meat tenderizer
* Garlic powder

Can be made the day before: allow to cool when finished cooking, slice meat. Put gravy in separate container and refrigerate both meat and gravy. Before heating to serve, skim fat off of gravy, reheat meat and gravy together at 300 degrees for 30 to 40 minutes.

Recipe Instructions

* Preheat oven to 250 degrees.
* Wash and dry roast.
* Rub with browning sauce of choice; sprinkle with meat tenderizer and garlic powder on both sides.
* Spray 9 x 13 inch glass dish with cooking spray and put roast in, add half to one cup water.
* Let stand at room temperature for one hour.
* Bake for five to six hours, basting every two hours and adding water when necessary to prevent drying of meat.

This is my all-time favorite meat that my mom makes. It is simply heaven!

Sweet and Sour Meatballs

Makes: 6 to 8 servings
Source: Mom

Ingredients

Sauce (make first):

* 1 12-ounce bottle chili sauce
* 1 16-ounce can jellied cranberry sauce
* 1 can water from cranberry sauce
* 2 small onions, finely chopped
* 2 teaspoons garlic powder
* 1/4 teaspoon fresh ginger
* 2 tablespoons fresh lemon juice
* 1/8 to 1/4 cup *matzo* meal

Meatballs:

* 2 pounds lean ground beef
* 1 egg, beaten
* 4 tablespoons ketchup
* 1/4 teaspoon salt
* 1/8 teaspoon pepper
* 2 teaspoons garlic powder
* 1/4 cup *matzo* meal

Recipe Instructions

Sauce:

* Mix all ingredients for sauce together in large Dutch oven and bring to boil.
* Reduce heat to a simmer and stir frequently to prevent burning.

Meatballs:

* Combine all ingredients for meatballs together in large bowl and mix well.
* Form meatballs about one inch in diameter and drop into simmering sauce one at a time. (Stir gently, as they break apart easily.)
* Cook covered for one hour, stirring every 10 minutes to prevent burning.

During Pesach, *depending upon customs, may serve with popover rolls (see recipe in* Pesach *section); on* Shabbat *and* chaggim *serve with* challah.

> There is just something about this recipe that creates sweet and delicious memories. The blend of tastes, the aroma while cooking, all lend to something special. This dish is the favorite of my second son and my step-son and I do my best to make it for them whenever we are all together. Although it is kosher for Passover, we enjoy it all year-round.

Ground Beef Favorites

Ma Catapan's Meatloaf

Makes: 4 to 6 servings
Source: Norma Marcin

Ingredients

* 2 pounds ground beef
* 1 cup bread crumbs
* 2 onions, finely chopped
* 2 eggs, beaten well
* 2 teaspoons salt
* 1/2 teaspoon pepper
* 4 8-ounce cans tomato sauce
* 1 cup water
* 6 tablespoons vinegar
* 6 tablespoons brown sugar
* 4 tablespoons yellow mustard
* 4 tablespoons Worcestershire® sauce

Recipe Instructions

* Preheat oven to 350 degrees.
* Mix together beef, crumbs, onions, egg, salt, pepper, and 8 ounces tomato sauce.
* Form into loaf and place in 9 x 13 inch glass or foil pan.
* Combine remaining ingredients in bowl, mix well, and pour over meatloaf.
* Bake for 1 hour and 15 minutes, basting every 15 minutes.
* Serve with flat noodles or on bread.

Chili Con Carne

Makes: 6 servings
Source: Mom

Ingredients

* 2 tablespoons oil
* 2 pounds lean ground beef
* 2 tablespoons flour
* 1/4 cup chopped onion
* 2 to 3 cloves garlic, minced
* 2 to 2-1/2 tablespoons chili powder
* 2 16-ounce cans Italian (cut up) or crushed tomatoes
* 1-1/2 cups water
* 2 cans red kidney beans, drained/rinsed
* 1-1/2 teaspoons Worcestershire® sauce
* 1/4 teaspoon Tabasco® sauce

Recipe Instructions

* Sprinkle meat with flour and mix.
* Sauté onions and garlic in oil until transparent; add meat and brown.
* Add chili powder, tomatoes, water, Tabasco®, Worcestershire® sauce, and beans.
* Cover and simmer for one hour, stirring to prevent burning, or bake in 350 degree oven for one hour in oven-proof pot.
* Serve with *pareve* oyster crackers.

Chili Con Carne

Iraqi Meatballs with Green Peas

Iraqi Meatballs with Green Peas

Makes: 6 to 8 servings
Source: Hana Manzur

Ingredients

Meatballs:

✣ 2 pounds lean ground beef
✣ 1 bunch parsley (approximately 1 cup, rinse well and check for bugs), finely chopped
✣ 1 onion, chopped
✣ 2 tablespoons salt, or to taste
✣ 2 tablespoons fresh black pepper, or to taste

Sauce:

✣ 1 tablespoon grapeseed oil
✣ 3 cups water
✣ 1-1/2 teaspoons dry chicken soup mix
✣ 1 teaspoon salt
✣ 1/4 teaspoon pepper, or to taste
✣ Tumeric to color light yellow
✣ 1/8 teaspoon curry
✣ 2 bay leaves
✣ 1 large bag frozen green peas

Recipe Instructions

✣ Combine ingredients for meatballs in large bowl and set aside to rest for 15 minutes.
✣ Form meatballs.
✣ Except for peas, combine sauce ingredients, bring to boil; add meatballs and cook covered for 25 minutes on medium heat, stirring gently once or twice during this time.
✣ Add frozen peas to pot.
✣ Continue to cook 20 to 30 minutes on medium heat, stirring occasionally.
✣ Serve with white rice.

Oma's Meat Spaghetti Sauce

Makes: 4 servings
Source: Oma

Ingredients

* 1 onion, chopped
* 1 tablespoon grapeseed oil
* 1 pound ground beef
* 1 16-ounce can stewed tomatoes
* 1 6-ounce can tomato paste
* 1 10-ounce can of *parve* tomato soup
* 2 cloves garlic, minced
* 2 tablespoon garlic powder
* 1/4 teaspoon salt
* 1/2 teaspoon basil
* 1/2 teaspoon oregano
* 1/8 teaspoon pepper
* 1 or 2 bay leaves
* 1/2 cup fresh, chopped mushrooms (optional)
* 1/2 tablespoon sugar

This recipe doubles or triples easily and tastes even better if refrigerated overnight and reheated and served the following day.

Recipe Instructions

* Brown onion in hot oil, add meat and cook until lightly browned. Push meat from side to side and skim off fat with paper towels.
* Add tomatoes, tomato paste, soup and seasonings, except for sugar.
* Simmer two hours, stirring occasionally, over low flame, or bake in oven at 325 degrees for two hours in oven-safe pot.
* Add sugar and adjust seasoning to taste.
* Serve over favorite type of pasta (during *Pesach* purchase kosher for Passover noodles).

> *Warmth and love over pasta. That's the only way I can define it.*

Oma's Meat Spaghetti Sauce

Oma's Rouladen with Red Cabbage

Oma's Rouladen

Makes: 8 servings
Source: Oma

Ingredients

✻ 8 4"x 6" pieces first-cut book steaks, cut from a book roast or shoulder roast sliced 1/4 inch thick
✻ 8 tablespoons stone-ground mustard
✻ 3/4 pound sliced raw beef fry
✻ 2 large onions, sliced in rings and then cut in half
✻ Kosher salt or sea salt
✻ 1/4 to 1/2 cup flour
✻ Freshly ground black pepper
✻ 1 cup dry red wine
✻ 1 cup cold water
✻ (1 tablespoon flour with 1/4 cup cold water to thicken gravy, if needed)

Also need:

✻ 6-quart enamel cast-iron pot with cover and thread or toothpicks to secure rouladen rolls
✻ Meat tenderizing hammer

Recipe Instructions

✻ Set aside eight slices of beef fry for rouladen rolls.
✻ Over low heat, spray pot with cooking spray and add two tablespoons canola oil.
✻ Cut remaining beef fry in small pieces and heat in pot, turning frequently to brown and release the fat, about 10 minutes. Turn off heat and set aside.
✻ Remove beef fry from pot before browning rouladen and add back to pot when ready to cook rouladen in the gravy.
✻ Place each piece of meat on a large cutting board covered in foil. Sprinkle generously with salt and pepper. Cover with plastic wrap and pound evenly
with hammer.
✻ Spread a half to one tablespoon of mustard thinly and evenly onto each piece of meat. At one end of meat, place piece of beef fry folded in half and two pieces of cut-up onion. Roll meat into traditional elongated shape and use toothpicks to secure or wrap with thread. Repeat with each remaining piece of meat.
✻ Dredge each rouladen in flour. Re-heat pot with oil over medium-high heat (adding oil when needed) and place rouladen in pot and brown using quarterturns to brown all sides

Continued...

(approximately two to three minutes each turn). Approximately four rouladen will fit in pot for browning at each time. Once complete, set aside and brown remaining rouladen.

❈ Turn heat to low. To deglaze pot, carefully add half cup of wine and one cup cold water to pot and loosen all the brown remains on bottom of pot with a wooden spoon; avoid burning.

❈ Place all rouladen in pot with deglazed gravy (they will fit snuggly). Add back the browned beef fry; cover tightly and cook over medium-low heat for about two hours (gravy should have small bubbles while cooking), checking every 30 minutes, to make sure there is enough liquid for cooking. If necessary, add water for additional liquid.

❈ When rolls are done, take out of pot and set aside.

❈ Add half cup wine to gravy and adjust with salt and pepper.

❈ To thicken, turn heat to medium; mix one tablespoon flour in a quarter cup water and add to gravy, stirring constantly until gravy boils and thickens. Return rouladen to gravy, cover and warm over low heat in gravy until ready to serve.

❈ Best served with Oma's Red Cabbage and Roasted Red Potatoes.

Rouladen is a special dish traditionally used as a German celebratory food. My Oma perfected this dish but never wrote down her exact recipe. My mom has successfully recreated her dish through memories and research. Here's to you, Oma!

Five-Star Minute Steak

Makes: 6 to 8 servings
Source: Shaul with adaptations by Mia

Ingredients

❖ 8 to 10 minute steaks
❖ 3 large onions, chopped
❖ 2 stalks celery, chopped
❖ 1 cup fresh chopped mushrooms
❖ 3 tablespoons onion soup mix
❖ 2 teaspoons ground black pepper (or to taste)
❖ 3 tablespoons olive oil
❖ 2 bulbs garlic, peeled and separated

Recipe Instructions

❖ Preheat oven to 325 degrees.
❖ Make 1/2" slit in center of each minute steak and place in metal or foil baking pan, one right next to the other.
❖ Stuff one or two cloves of garlic into slit of each steak; throw any additional garlic into the pan.
❖ Create bed of chopped onions on top of steaks.
❖ Evenly spread chopped celery on top of onions.
❖ Evenly spread sliced mushrooms on top of celery.
❖ Sprinkle onion soup mix across top of vegetables.
❖ Sprinkle black pepper across top of vegetables.
❖ Pour olive oil over top of vegetables.
❖ Seal pan tightly with aluminum foil.
❖ Bake for three to four hours until steaks are very tender, checking hourly for adequate liquid in pan (add water if necessary to prevent drying).
❖ Serve over bed of rice (some do not eat rice on *Pesach* so omit).

Of all the meat recipes that I make, this one receives the most compliments. Fortunately, it is fairly simple to make and unfortunately, there are never any leftovers!

Bambia

Makes: 6 to 8 servings
Source: Hana Manzur

Ingredients

✤ 2 pounds lean ground beef
✤ 2 26-ounce jars tomato sauce of choice
✤ Frozen okra (2 bags of large okra or 3 bags of baby okra)
✤ 2 tablespoons sugar
✤ Juice of 1 lemon
✤ 2 to 3 tablespoons each salt and pepper, or to taste
✤ 5 medium to large onions, chopped
✤ 3 tablespoons tumeric
✤ 1 jar water (jar from tomato sauce)
✤ 2 to 3 tablespoons grapeseed oil

This is one of the first Iraqi dishes that my husband taught me how to make. I had never eaten okra before and was fairly certain my kids would reject it. Much to my surprise, not only did the kids love it but it has become a favorite!

Recipe Instructions

To prepare meatballs:

✤ Combine a quarter cup of chopped onions in large bowl with ground beef, one tablespoon salt and one tablespoon pepper.
✤ Blend thoroughly, then form into small meatballs.

In large pot on stove:

✤ Over high heat, add grapeseed oil to cover bottom of pot, and add remaining onions. Sauté until onions almost soft.
✤ Begin adding meatballs into bottom of pot on top of onions, and allow to brown.
✤ Stir the onions and meatballs gently to prevent burning.
✤ Once meatballs are browned, add: tomato sauce, sugar, juice of lemon, tumeric, remaining salt and pepper, water, and okra.
✤ Stir until blended; cover and cook on medium heat until bubbling, stirring every 5 to 10 minutes to prevent burning.
✤ Simmer over medium-low heat, covered, for one hour, stirring every 15 minutes.
✤ Adjust seasoning to taste while cooking.
✤ Serve with rice (some do not eat rice on *Pesach*, so omit accordingly).

Brisket and Onions

Makes: 6 servings
Source: Marcy Rotenberg

Ingredients

✤ First cut of beef brisket, 4 to 5 pounds
✤ 2 large red onions and 2 large white onions, sliced thin
✤ 5 cloves garlic, peeled and sliced in half
✤ 1 cup sweet white wine
✤ 1 package onion soup mix
✤ Coarse salt and ground pepper
✤ 2 cups low-sodium chicken broth
✤ 3 tablespoons oil

Recipe Instructions

✤ Heat slow-cooker on low.
✤ Rub each side of meat with salt, pepper, and onion soup mix.
✤ Heat oil in pan and brown meat on both sides.
✤ Remove meat once browned and set aside.
✤ In same pan sauté onions and garlic stirring frequently to prevent burning. Add oil if necessary.
✤ Once onions and garlic are browned, remove and place in bed of slow cooker.
✤ Place meat on top of onions.
✤ Deglaze pan by adding small amount of chicken broth; once particles have released from bottom of pan pour liquid over the meat.
✤ Add chicken broth and white wine.
✤ Cover slow-cooker and leave to cook for minimum of six hours on low heat. Larger pieces of meat will require longer cooking times. (Tip: Can be put into slow-cooker before bedtime and left to cook overnight.)
✤ Prior to cutting, remove meat from slow-cooker and allow to rest and cool 15 to 30 minutes.
✤ Cut meat, place in serving or storage dish, add onions, garlic, and sauce to serving or storage dish from slow-cooker to serve immediately or store and reheat.

Mia's Mustard Braised Brisket

Makes: 10-12 people
Source: Mia

Ingredients

✤ 4 1/2 pound brisket, 1st cut (or whatever size you wish—cook approx. 1.25-1.5 hours per pound)
✤ Preferred mustard (I use Emeril's Kicked Up Horseradish Mustard All Natural)
✤ Freshly ground black pepper
✤ Kosher salt
✤ 2-3 tablespoons olive oil
✤ 10 garlic cloves peeled
✤ 1 1/2 cups red wine (I use Baron Herzog Jeunesse Cabernet Sauvignon)
✤ 3 cups beef broth
✤ 1 1/2 tablespoons unbleached all-purpose flour
✤ 2 yellow onions, thinly sliced
✤ 1 tablespoons hot water or wine

Recipe Instructions

✤ Rub the brisket all over generously with the mustard on both sides of meat, wrap in plastic wrap, and refrigerate overnight.
✤ Season both sides of the meat liberally with salt and pepper. Heat the olive oil over medium-heat in a Dutch oven. When the oil shimmers, brown the meat on all sides.
✤ Remove the meat from pan and set aside. Add the onions and garlic to the pan (you may need to add an additional tablespoon of olive oil if the pan is too dry). Sauté just until slightly softened, about 1 minute. Deglaze with 1 tablespoon hot water or wine, scraping up all the brown bits from the bottom of the pan.
✤ Place the brisket back in the pot on top of onions and garlic, along with the red wine and beef broth. Bring to a boil, then reduce to a simmer. Cover the pot, and simmer for 6 hours. It is recommended to use a *blech*, or protective heat plate, under the pan to prevent burning. Check liquid and baste meat every hour. Liquid should reach up to sides of meat during cooking.
✤ After 6 hours, remove meat and set aside to rest until at room temperature.
✤ Using potato masher, mash all contents in remaining liquid in pan. Boil the liquid in the Dutch oven vigorously until 4 cups of liquid remain.

Continued...

✻ Using a glass measuring cup, remove one cup of liquid from pan, add flour to cup and mix thoroughly breaking down any clumps of flower. Once blended, return cup of liquid to pan, increase heat back to a boil, and stir consistently until texture of liquid thickens slightly. Remove pan from heat and let sit while preparing meat.

✻ Once meat is at room temperature, slice and place in dish that can be heated. At this time you can either add the gravy back to the pan with the meat in order to heat for eating that night, or you can store meat and gravy separately until ready to heat and use at a later time.

Lauren's Sloppy Joes

Makes: 6 to 8 servings
Source: Lauren Groveman

Ingredients

Sauce:

❈ 3 tablespoons oil
❈ 1 cup packed minced yellow onion
❈ 1/2 cup packed seeded and minced green bell pepper
❈ 1/4 cup seeded and minced red bell pepper
❈ 2 tablespoons minced celery
❈ 6 cloves garlic, minced
❈ 2 cups canned tomato purée
❈ 2 rounded tablespoons tomato paste
❈ 1 cup ketchup
❈ 2 tablespoons cider vinegar
❈ 1/4 cup unsulphered molasses
❈ 2 teaspoons Worcestershire® sauce
❈ 1 tablespoon extra-virgin olive oil
❈ 1 cup chopped, clean, fresh button mushrooms or Portobello mushroom caps
❈ 1-1/2 cups peeled, seeded, and coarsely chopped ripe plum tomatoes
❈ 1 teaspoon crumbled dried oregano
❈ 1 teaspoon beef bouillon
❈ Freshly ground black pepper, to taste

For Remainder of Dish:

❈ 2 generous cups of previously made sauce
❈ 2 generous pounds freshly ground beef (chuck, round, or combination) or ground veal or turkey
❈ Freshly ground black pepper to taste
❈ 6 to 8 large hamburger buns
❈ Extra-virgin olive oil
❈ Minced garlic
❈ Italian parsley, chopped, for the buns

Continued...

Recipe Instructions

❉ To start sauce: Heat a 2 1/2 quart, saucepan over medium heat. When hot, add the oil.

❉ When oil is hot, stir in onion, green and red peppers, celery and garlic. Cook until vegetables are softened and fragrant (four to five minutes).

❉ Stir in tomato purée, tomato paste, ketchup, vinegar, molasses and Worcestershire® sauce. Bring mixture to simmer; reduce heat to very low and simmer with cover ajar for one hour.

❉ To sauté mushrooms, heat an eight-inch skillet over high heat.

❉ Once hot, add the oil–when oil is hot, add chopped mushrooms and cook, stirring frequently, until mushrooms are golden (two to three minutes); remove from heat and set aside.

❉ To finish the sauce, after sauce has simmered one hour, add sautéed mushrooms, chopped plum tomatoes, oregano, bouillon, and fresh ground pepper; return to simmer and cook with cover ajar for 30 minutes.

❉ If using right away, take desired sauce and allow remainder to cool. Freeze cooled sauce in tightly sealed containers.

❉ Brown ground meat. Remove any excess fat from skillet, and return to low flame on stove.

❉ Stir in prepared sauce and bring mixture to simmer, uncovered. Cook gently until flavors mingle and mixture is hot throughout (about 10 minutes). Add black pepper to taste and serve immediately.

❉ To serve: while mixture is simmering, open hamburger buns and spread both open sides lightly with olive oil that has been mixed with minced garlic and chopped parsley. Lay buns seasoned side up on baking sheet and broil until nicely toasted.

❉ Spoon ground beef mixture lavishly over buns and serve hot.

❉ During *Pesach*, depending upon customs, may serve over *Pesach* popover rolls instead of buns (recipe found in *Pesach* section).

> *Aside from this being an amazing recipe, Lauren is the one who truly helped me bring food and cooking into my heart. She took me under her wing and taught me with love how to expand my cooking horizons. I am so thankful for her generosity of spirit and kindness of heart—and, of course, her delicious recipes!*

Boeuf Bourguignon

Makes: 6 servings
Source: Executive Chef/Author
Laura Frankel

Ingredients

* 2 pounds of beef chuck-cut into 2 inch pieces
* Olive oil
* 2 carrots, peeled and cut into 1 inch pieces
* 2 medium Spanish onions, diced
* 4 cloves of garlic, peeled and chopped
* 2 celery ribs
* 2 tablespoons tomato paste
* 2 cups red wine (I like a hearty Pinot Noir)
* 1 cup of chicken stock
* Bouquet Garni (fragrant bouquet) of: several sprigs of thyme, parsley stems, whole cloves, 1 bay leaf
* 1 pound mushrooms (cremini, button or shiitake), quartered
* 1 cup pearl onions, blanched, shocked (stop the cooking process by quickly putting the food in ice water) and peeled
* Cheesecloth
* Kitchen twine

Recipe Instructions

* Preheat oven to 300 degrees.
* Heat a large sauté pan over medium high heat. Lightly coat the bottom of the pan with olive oil. Brown the meat on all sides in batches until the meat is dark brown (about 3-5 minutes per side).
* Remove the browned pieces and continue until all the meat is browned. Do not overcrowd the pan or the meat will not brown, but cook instead.
* Add the vegetables to the same pan, adding more oil if necessary, and cook until they are browned (about 10 minutes).
* Add the chopped garlic and continue to cook for 5 more minutes until the garlic is very fragrant and slightly softened. Remove the vegetables from the pan and set aside.
* Add the wine to the pan and deglaze the pan by scraping up the browned bits that are stuck to the bottom of the pan (the brown bits have tons of flavor-don't lose it!) with a wooden spoon or spatula.
* Reduce the wine by 1/2 (this concentrates the flavor by cooking the water out of it. This can also thicken the liquid as well and intensify the flavor.) . Add the tomato paste and chicken stock.
* Place the meat and vegetables in a large

Continued...

Dutch oven or casserole with a lid. Pour the wine over the meat.
❖ Wrap the celery, thyme sprigs, parsley stems, bay leaf and whole cloves into a bundle in the cheesecloth. Secure the bundle with kitchen twine. Add the bouquet garni to the Dutch oven.
❖ Braise the beef until it is tender and releases easily when pierced with a fork (about 2 1/2-3 hours).
❖ Gently remove the beef from the Dutch oven and set aside. Discard the vegetables and bouquet garnish.
❖ Reduce the braising liquid over medium high heat, stirring occasionally, until it is reduced by 1/2 until it is thick and coats the back of a spoon.
❖ Sauté the mushrooms and pearl onions until lightly browned and caramelized (about 5-7 minutes).
❖ Add the mushrooms, onions and beef back to the reduced braising liquid and serve. Garnish with chopped parsley. Serve with pasta, rice or mashed potatoes.

> *Laura is truly an inspiration to me. She has worked so hard and achieved so much not just as any chef, but as a woman chef in a male-dominated industry. She works side-by-side with world-famous chef Wolfgang Puck and is one of the key people in his organization. I have observed her through the years as she pioneered the opening of a five-star kosher restaurant in Chicago, with an eye and heart for only the best, taking kosher cuisine to an entirely new level. Her cookbooks are fun and easy to use. I feel so lucky to be able to have her as a role model, not just in the cooking world, but as a female entrepreneur who has truly risen above the pack. Thank you Laura!*

Poultry

"One of the most important responsibilities a woman has is to keep a kosher kitchen. The reason for this is self-evident: generally speaking, husbands are not home enough hours in the day... and even if given the necessary time, they do not have the necessary skills or patience to do so."

Rabbi Yossef Haim, z"l
"Ben Ish Chai"

Chicken Wings Mandarin

Makes: 4 to 6 servings
Source: Mom

Ingredients

❖ 15 to 18 chicken wings, remove tips and cut in half at joint
❖ Grapeseed oil
❖ 1 cup cornstarch
❖ 2 eggs, beaten
❖ 1/4 teaspoon salt
❖ 1/4 teaspoon garlic powder
❖ 1/4 teaspoon seasoned salt
❖ 1/4 to 1/2 cup cold water

Recipe Instructions

❖ Cut, wash and dry chicken wings.
❖ Combine ingredients (except for oil), adding the quarter cup to half cup cold water to make the batter of medium consistency. Stir lightly.
❖ Coat wings with batter and fry in hot grapeseed oil until light brown; drain on paper towels.

Chicken with 40 Cloves Garlic

Makes: 4 servings
Source: Nina Deitch

Ingredients

✤ 1 3-pound frying chicken, cut up or 4 breasts with bones
✤ 4 heads of garlic, broken into cloves (about 40 unpeeled)
✤ 1/2 cup olive oil
✤ 1 tablespoon dried thyme
✤ 1 tablespoon dried oregano
✤ 1 tablespoon marjoram
✤ Salt and pepper, to taste
✤ French bread

Recipe Instructions

✤ Preheat oven to 350 degrees.
✤ Toss chicken pieces and garlic cloves with oil and spices and place into cast iron enameled casserole or glass dish; salt and pepper to taste.
✤ Cover and bake for one and a half hours.
✤ Cut French bread in half and bake in oven for 10 minutes.
✤ Serve chicken and garlic from casserole, dipping bread into pan juices and squeezing garlic out of skin to spread on bread.
✤ During *Pesach*, depending upon customs, may serve with *Pesach* popover rolls instead of French bread (recipe found in *Pesach* section).

Stir Fry Chicken

Stir Fry Chicken

Makes: 6 servings
Source: Mia

Ingredients

❖ Large wok or frying skillet
❖ 5 pounds of boneless, skinless chicken breast, cut in bite-size pieces
❖ 1 red bell pepper, seeded and sliced long
❖ 1 large onion, chopped
❖ 4 cloves garlic, halved
❖ Fresh Portabello mushrooms, sliced long
❖ Soy sauce, black pepper, garlic powder, and salt to taste
❖ 6 tablespoons grapeseed oil
❖ 1/2 cup chopped broccoli
❖ 1/2 cup chopped celery
❖ 1/2 cup chopped spinach
❖ (Wash and check all vegetables for bugs)

Recipe Instructions

❖ In large bowl, place cut chicken and add soy sauce, pepper, garlic powder and a touch salt; add enough of each to cover (but not saturate) the top of the chicken pile. Mix throughly and set aside.
❖ Heat four tablespoons oil in wok on medium-high heat.
❖ Add chicken to wok and cook, stirring frequently for approximately 10 minutes, until exterior of chicken pieces appear cooked (inside will not be cooked through), then remove from wok and set aside in clean bowl.
❖ Heat two tablespoons oil on medium-high heat and add all vegetables to wok. Cook for 10 minutes, stirring frequently.
❖ Return chicken to wok and cook all ingredients together, adjusting seasonings to taste. Cook until chicken is cooked through, stirring frequently to avoid burning.
❖ Serve over bed of white or brown rice or pasta (some do not eat soy, rice, or Passover pastas on *Pesach*, so omit accordingly).

Chicken on the Sweet Side

Saphi's Chicken

Makes: 3 to 4 servings
Source: Mom

Ingredients

* 1 cut-up frying chicken or 4 chicken breasts on the bone
* 8-ounce bottle *pareve* Russian salad dressing
* 1 cup apricot jam
* 6 tablespoons *pareve* onion soup mix
* 1/2 teaspoon garlic powder

Recipe Instructions

* Preheat oven to 350 degrees.
* Spray shallow pan (foil or glass) with cooking spray.
* Mix everything but the chicken together.
* Place chicken in pan and pour mixture over chicken.
* Bake uncovered for one and a half hours, turning and basting every 30 minutes.

Honey Mustard Chicken

Makes: 3 to 4 servings
Source: Nina Deitch

Ingredients

* 1/2 cup honey
* 1/2 cup Dijon mustard
* 1/2 to 1-1/2 teaspoons curry
* 1 teaspoon minced garlic, fresh
* 2 tablespoon soy sauce
* 1 chicken, cut up or 4 chicken breasts on the bone

Recipe Instructions

* Preheat oven to 350 degrees.
* Except for chicken, combine all ingredients in a bowl and mix well.
* In a 9 x 13-inch glass dish, lay out chicken pieces and pour mixture over chicken.
* Marinate chicken pieces for at least four hours (overnight in refrigerator is preferred), turning periodically and basting with mixture.
* Place dish in oven and cook uncovered for about one hour, until chicken is cooked through, basting occasionally.

Honey Mustard Chicken

Whole Chicken Baked on Kosher Salt

Makes: 3 to 4 servings
Source: Mom

Ingredients

✤ Large whole chicken
✤ Coarse Kosher salt
✤ Whole head of garlic (optional), with papery outer skin peeled off

Recipe Instructions

✤ Preheat oven to 325 degrees.
✤ Wash and dry chicken and trim any visible fat.
✤ Line a shallow baking pan with heavy-duty foil, shiny side up.
✤ Completely cover bottom of pan with kosher salt, creating a bed of salt.
✤ Place whole chicken on bed of salt, back side down, breast side up.
✤ Stuff whole head of garlic into cavity of chicken.
✤ Bake for three to three and a half hours.
✤ Remove from oven and let rest five to 10 minutes, then cut and serve.
✤ Garlic bulbs can be spread onto bread (or *matzo* during *Pesach*) or eaten with chicken.

> *Could not be more simple, could not be more delicious. This is the go-to meal for those busy days when cooking is going to be a challenge. Also is fantastic for cooling and saving the meat for chicken salads.*

Chicken Sepharadi

Makes: 3 to 4 servings
Source: Hana Manzur

Ingredients

✤ 1 whole chicken, cleaned and cut in eighths
✤ 1 to 2 teaspoons poultry seasoning
✤ 1 10-3/4-ounce can tomato-mushroom sauce
✤ 1 medium onion
✤ 1 medium green pepper
✤ 1/2 cup green olives
✤ 1/2 cup red wine, dry

Recipe Instructions

✤ In a large 6 or 8 quart pot arrange chicken pieces skin side up.
✤ Season with poultry seasoning. Slice onions and green peppers into circles and place on top of chicken.
✤ Place approximately half cup (or to taste) of green olives on top of chicken and pour tomato-mushroom sauce on top of chicken.
✤ Cook covered for one hour on medium-low heat, basting every 15 minutes.
✤ After 45 minutes of baking, pour half cup dry red wine over chicken. Reduce heat if necessary to prevent burning.
✤ Serve from baking dish with white rice as a side (some do not eat rice on *Pesach* so omit).

This is one of my father-in-law's favorite dishes that I make. I always make extra so that he can take some home and enjoy the next day.

Tabit
(Sepharadi Chicken and Rice)

Makes: 6 to 8 servings
Source: Shaul

Ingredients

* 1 whole roasting chicken
* 3 cups rice
* 2 onions, chopped
* 2 tomatoes, puréed
* 2 tablespoons cardamom
* 2 tablespoons baharat (a Middle Eastern spice)
* 2 tablespoons salt
* 2 tablespoons black pepper
* Boiling water as needed
* 1 tablespoon olive oil

Recipe Instructions

* Wash rice three times with hot water and then let soak for two hours.
* Drain rice and place at bottom of large pot over medium-low flame.
* In skillet, sauté onions and add to rice; continue cooking and stirring.
* Add tomato purée, half of all spices and enough water to just cover the stew.
* Cook rice mixture over medium-low flame until half-cooked (approximately 20 minutes) and then add chicken on top of mixture.
* Add second half of all spices and olive oil over chicken and cook covered over low heat for several hours until cooked, or cook overnight.
* It is important to periodically add water to prevent burning or drying out.
* If making for *Shabbat*, be sure flame is on lowest setting and when adding water on *Shabbat*, the water must be hot water from the kettle in order to not violate the laws of *Shabbat*.

Fish

*"Give a man a fish and you feed him for a day.
Teach a man to fish and you feed him for a lifetime."*

Maimonides

Simple Salmon

Makes: 6 to 8 servings
Source: Mia

Ingredients

✤ 3 to 4 pounds wild-caught salmon, with skin, cut in 1-1/2-inch wide pieces
✤ Salt, pepper, garlic powder and paprika to taste
✤ 2 large lemons, one sliced to garnish top of fish and the other for juice
✤ Cooking spray

Recipe Instructions

✤ Preheat oven to 325 degrees.
✤ Place fish pieces skin-side down on foil-lined baking pan that has been sprayed with cooking spray (to prevent sticking).
✤ Lightly squeeze juice of one lemon over all pieces of fish; remove any fallen seeds.
✤ Dust pieces of fish with spices, to taste.
✤ Garnish top of fish with lemon slices.
✤ Bake for 12 to 20 minutes, until fish is at desired firmness.
✤ Serve on bed of lettuce with garnishing vegetables or over bed of rice with touch of soy sauce (some do not eat rice or soy sauce on *Pesach* so omit accordingly).

Gefilte Fish

Makes: 15 servings
Source: Bubby Irma

Ingredients

* 1 pound ground fish (carp, silver carp, or whitefish and pike)
* 1/2 cup *matzo* meal
* Black pepper, to taste
* 4 tablespoons salt
* 6 tablespoons sugar
* 2 eggs
* 1 carrot
* 3 onions
* Oil

Recipe Instructions

* Slice two onions, sauté in small amount of oil in frying pan over low flame until soft and translucent, but not brown.
* Grind sautéed onions and mix well with ground fish.
* Add *matzo* meal, eggs, three tablespoons sugar, two tablespoons salt and pepper and let stand 15 minutes.
* Fill a medium pot halfway with water, add sliced carrot, one sliced onion, two tablespoons salt, three tablespoons sugar and black pepper and bring to boil.
* Make fish balls with wet hands; place the balls into the simmering stock; cook for 45 minutes, partially covered.
* When cooled, pour the sauce into a jar and refrigerate until it gels. Use gel to garnish; place fish in covered container and chill.
* Serve fish cold with horseradish and/or parsley and/or cooked carrots.

Variation: Spicy Baked Gefilte Fish

* Combine half cup tomato sauce, half cup water, salt and pepper to taste.
* Pour over cooked gefilte fish pieces in baking dish and bake half-hour at 350 degrees.

Gefilte Fish

Moroccan Fish

Moroccan Fish

Makes: 6 to 8 servings
Source: Shaul

Ingredients

* 3 to 4 pounds wild-caught salmon, skinned, sliced into 1-1/2-inch thick pieces
* 3 bell peppers, cut thin
* 1 bulb garlic, cleaned and cloves cut in half
* 1/2 large onion, cut in thin rings and then halved
* 1 can tomato sauce
* 1/2 cup water
* 1 to 2 teaspoons each: salt, black pepper, turmeric and curry, or to taste
* 1 teaspoon *Schug* (chopped and seasoned spiced pepper found in refrigerator section of most kosher stores) or equivalent
* 1 large lemon, 1/2 sliced thin, other 1/2 for squeezing juice
* 1 can garbanzo beans (chick peas)
* 1/2 bag (about 8 ounces) baby carrots, sliced long
* 2 tablespoons grapeseed oil

Recipe Instructions

* In large stock pot, sauté bell peppers, garlic, and onion in grapeseed oil, over medium heat.
* Add tomato sauce and water, stir.
* Add salt, black pepper, and one rounded teaspoon *Schug*; stir.
* Add turmeric and touch of curry.
* Add thin slices of lemon and squeeze second half of lemon into pot (remove any seeds that fall).
* Add garbanzo beans, stir.
* Add carrots, stir.
* Prepare fish while sauce cooks until well heated (about 10 minutes).
* Gently add fish pieces to pot; stir gently to be sure fish is covered.
* Cook covered for 40 to 50 minutes over medium-low heat, stirring occasionally to avoid burning, until carrots are soft.

The most amazing fish dish that I know how to prepare. It is light, healthy, flavorful, and can be served hot or cold. This also happens to be one of my husband's favorites.

Fish Salads

Tuna Salad

Makes: 4 to 6 servings
Source: Mom

Ingredients

* 1 13-ounce can solid white tuna
* 4 hard boiled eggs
* 2 green onions (scallions)
* 1/2 small white onion
* 2 to 3 pieces celery
* Mayonnaise, for taste and texture
* Sweet pickle relish, to taste

Recipe Instructions

* Chop eggs, onions and celery.
* Add all ingredients together, mix well and chill before serving.

Salmon Salad

Makes: 6 servings
Source: Mom

Ingredients

* 2 14-1/2-ounce cans canned salmon, cleaned
* 1 cup mayonnaise
* 1 tablespoon lemon juice
* 1 packet sugar substitute
* 1 tablespoon vinegar
* 1 tablespoon onion (chopped green or dried)
* 1 tablespoon dried celery (or 3 tablespoons fresh celery)
* 4 teaspoons brown mustard
* 4 teaspoons horseradish
* 1-1/2 teaspoons dried dill

Recipe Instructions

* Mix all ingredients well and refrigerate.
* Serve with bagels, crackers, etc.
* During *Pesach* serve with *matzo* crackers.

Vegetables

*"If you eat the fruit of the labor of your hands,
you will be happy and prosperous."*

Psalms (*Tehillim*)128:2

Oma's Red Cabbage

Makes: 10 servings
Source: Oma

Ingredients

✣ 8 8-ounce packages shredded cabbage or 2 small heads of red cabbage, shredded (check for bugs)
✣ 8 medium apples, unpeeled, cored and sliced in food processor
✣ 2 large yellow onions, chopped (used separately)
✣ 2 tablespoons canola oil
✣ 1 8-ounce package beef fry, cut into small pieces
✣ 3 large or 5 small bay leaves
✣ 2 cups chicken or vegetable stock
✣ 3/4 teaspoon fresh ground pepper
✣ 1 teaspoon ground cloves
✣ 2 tablespoons salt
✣ 1 cup vinegar
✣ 4 to 8 tablespoons brown sugar (if needed)

Tastes best if made the day before serving, refrigerated and then slowly reheated on stove top prior to serving.

Recipe Instructions

✣ Prepare red cabbage, apples, and onions and set aside.
✣ In large stainless steel pot (20-quart recommended), heat oil and add cut-up beef fry, cooking slowly over low heat.
✣ When there is little fat to be seen on the beef, add one chopped onion to beef fry and sauté about 10 minutes.
✣ Layer twice: half of the chopped cabbage, half of the apples, half of the remaining onion until all is added. Pot will be full, but will cook down to half (can put trivet under pot to prevent burning).
✣ Lay bay leaves on top; add two cups stock, pepper, ground cloves and salt.
✣ Turn heat to medium and let everything cook uncovered until color of cabbage turns pale and mixture starts to boil (usually about one and a half hours or more). Stir every 15 minutes, bringing up cabbage from bottom.
✣ Add one cup vinegar and cook for 30 minutes, partially cover and stir occasionally.
✣ Adjust salt, pepper, and vinegar to taste; add four to eight tablespoons brown sugar if too tart.

Oma's red cabbage dish is straight from "the old country." A well-known favorite in Germany, this dish is simply addictive. I have a funny memory from when I was about 10 years old: my Oma had just finished making the red cabbage and left the pot on the stove to cool while she went for a walk. The smell was divine! My mom and I simply couldn't resist and we snuck a huge bowl of the cabbage from the pot and sat on the couch sharing it and enjoying. When Oma returned she noticed the cabbage in the pot looked a bit less than when she had left. Needless to say my mom and I started laughing and Oma knew what had happened. Fortunately, it always made her happy when we ate her food so she took it as a big compliment and we didn't get in trouble!

Oma's Red Cabbage photo on Page 64 (with Oma's Rouladen)

Baked Sweet Potatoes

Makes: 3 to 4 servings
Source: Mom

Ingredients

✤ 1 40-ounce can sweet potatoes, save liquid
✤ 1 11-ounce can mandarin oranges, save liquid
✤ 6 shakes ground cinnamon
✤ 3 shakes ground cloves

Recipe Instructions

✤ Preheat oven to 350 degrees.
✤ Drain liquid from potatoes and oranges, and heat liquid in saucepan to boil.
✤ Add cinnamon and cloves to saucepan and simmer uncovered to reduce liquid, about 20 minutes.
✤ In a 9 x 9 inch baking dish, put potatoes and oranges and then pour liquid mixture over top.
✤ Bake for one hour.

Scalloped Corn Casserole

Makes: 4 to 6 servings
Source: Karen Koreba

Ingredients

✣ 2 tablespoons margarine (*pareve*) or butter (dairy)
✣ 1 16-ounce can creamed corn
✣ 1 16-ounce can corn kernels, drained
✣ 2 tablespoons cracker/bread crumbs
✣ 2 eggs, well beaten
✣ 1/4 teaspoon ground black pepper
✣ Pinch of salt
✣ 1/2 teaspoon sugar

Recipe Instructions

✣ Preheat oven to 375 degrees.
✣ Put margarine in one-quart loaf pan or glass baking dish and place in oven to melt.
✣ Remove and stir in corn, crumbs, salt, pepper, and sugar.
✣ Add eggs and mix thoroughly.
✣ Bake until firm and lightly browned on top (approximately 30 to 40 minutes).

Sweet Potato Casserole

Sweet Potato Casserole

Makes: 6 to 8 servings
Source: Karen Koreba

Ingredients

Dish:

* 3 cups baked sweet potatoes or 2 40-ounce cans sweet potatoes
* 1/3 cup sugar
* 1/2 teaspoon salt
* 2 eggs, beaten
* 1/2 stick margarine, melted
* 1/2 cup milk (for dairy) or non-dairy creamer (for *pareve*)
* 1/2 teaspoon vanilla

Topping:

* 1 cup brown sugar
* 1/3 cup flour
* 1 cup chopped walnuts or pecans
* 1/2 stick margarine, melted

Recipe Instructions

* Preheat oven to 350 degrees.
* Mash sweet potatoes with masher; add and mix the remaining ingredients one at a time, until fluffy.
* Pour into two-quart baking dish.
* In separate bowl, combine topping ingredients, mix well, and pour over sweet potato mixture.
* Bake for 35 minutes.

Unbelievable dish. Cannot celebrate Thanksgiving without it!

Roasted Veggies

Roasted Garlic

Makes: 3 to 4 servings
Source: Norman Van Aken

Ingredients

* 6 to 8 bulbs fresh garlic
* Good quality olive oil, to cover
* 1 to 1-1/2 tablespoons mixture of fresh thyme and rosemary in equal amounts
* 1 bay leaf
* 6 black peppercorns

Recipe Instructions

* Preheat oven to 300 degrees.
* Cut off tips of garlic bulbs; peel off papery outer skin.
* Arrange garlic bulbs, root side down, in pan just large enough to hold them fitting snugly.
* Pour oil over garlic and scatter the herbs onto the oil; add bay leaf and peppercorns.
* Cover with foil and bake 30 minutes, then uncover and baste.
* Replace foil and bake at 275 degrees for 30 more minutes.
* Take bulbs out of oil and put in pan to cool or serve warm.
* Delicious spread onto bread or served in salads, or during *Pesach* spread over *matzo*.

Roasted Red Potatoes

Makes: 4 servings
Source: Mom

Ingredients

* 12 small red potatoes, halved
* 4 scallions, chopped
* 2 tablespoons cooking oil
* Salt, garlic powder, and pepper to taste
* Cooking spray

Recipe Instructions

* Preheat oven to 400 degrees.
* Put cut-up potatoes in plastic bag, add oil and toss until potatoes are covered.
* Spray a 9 x 13 inch baking dish with cooking spray and put potatoes in dish.
* Sprinkle generously with salt, garlic powder, and pepper, to taste.
* Lay chopped green onions evenly across top.
* Bake uncovered for 45 to 75 minutes, until tender and light brown, turning potatoes with spatula every 30 minutes and adding spices as desired.

Roasted Garlic

Glazed Carrots

Simple but Delicious Veggies

Glazed Carrots

Makes: 8 servings
Source: Mom

Ingredients
* 2 pounds baby carrots
* 1/4 cup low-sugar apricot jam

Recipe Instructions
* Wash carrots and cut to small size, if necessary.
* Cook covered in steamer basket (put one inch of water in bottom of pot) for 10 to 12 minutes. Drain and return to pot. Drape top of pot with paper towel and cover with lid.
* In separate pot heat jam to simmer, pour over carrots and stir until they are glazed; cook over low heat, about three minutes.

Baked Onions

Makes: 6 servings
Source: Mom

Ingredients
* 6 onions, peeled, but leave stem on
* 8 to 10 tablespoons margarine (*pareve*), butter (dairy), or oil (margarine/butter if serving hot, oil if serving cold)
* Salt and pepper to taste

Recipe Instructions
* Preheat oven to 400 degrees.
* Put onions in baking dish; add margarine or oil. Sprinkle with salt and pepper.
* Bake for 45 minutes to one hour.

Vegetables ❋ 111

Soups

"Worries go down better with soup than without."

Jewish Proverb

French Onion Soup

Makes: 4 servings
Source: Recipe courtesy of Jaime Geller, *Quick & Kosher Recipes from the Bride Who Knew Nothing*

Ingredients

* 4 large onions, sliced
* 4 tablespoons butter (dairy) or margarine (*pareve*)
* 1 cup dry white wine
* 2 tablespoons flour
* 8 cups water
* 3 tablespoons onion soup mix
* 1 teaspoon salt
* 1/2 teaspoon black pepper
* French bread, sliced and toasted
* Gruyère cheese (or substitute with Swiss cheese if cannot find kosher Gruyère)

For Pareve: *substitute margarine for butter and omit cheese. The onion soup is excellent with or without the cheese topping.*
For KP: *omit French bread.*

Recipe Instructions

* In a four-quart stockpot, sauté onions in butter over medium heat for about eight minutes, or until carmelized to a nice golden brown, stirring frequently to avoid burning.
* Add wine and continue to sauté for two to three minutes.
* Slowly stir in flour.
* Stirring to keep lumps from forming; add water, onion soup mix, salt, and pepper; bring to boil over high heat.
* Reduce heat to low, cover, and simmer for one hour and 30 minutes.
* Place oven-safe serving bowls onto baking pan, ladle into bowls and place a piece of toasted French bread in each.
* Top the toast with a slice or two of cheese and broil for three minutes, until cheese is browned and bubbly.

Fantastic kosher version of this famous soup. Highly recommend it!

French Onion Soup

Asian Shiitake Mushroom Soup

Makes: 4 to 6 servings
Source: Recipe courtesy of Jaime Geller, *Quick & Kosher Recipes from the Bride Who Knew Nothing*

Ingredients

❖ 2 3-1/2-ounce cartons sliced shiitake mushrooms
❖ 6 cups water
❖ 2 cups chicken broth (meat), or broth of your choice (vegetable broth makes it *pareve*)
❖ 3/4 cup dry white wine
❖ 1 leek, washed and sliced, use just white part, about 1/2 cup
❖ 2 teaspoons grated fresh ginger (or 1 teaspoon ground ginger)
❖ 1-1/2 teaspoons toasted sesame oil
❖ 1/4 cup fresh minced parsley (or 1 tablespoon dried parsley)
❖ 1 tablespoon minced fresh dill (or 1 teaspoon dried dill)
❖ 4 frozen crushed garlic cubes
❖ 1/2 teaspoon sea salt

Recipe Instructions

❖ Place all ingredients in a six-quart stockpot.
❖ Cover and bring to boil.
❖ Reduce to a simmer and cook for 50 minutes.
❖ Ladle into bowls and serve.

Leek, Carrot, and Potato Soup

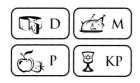

Makes: 6 servings
Source: Nina Deitch

Ingredients

❊ 1/2 stick margarine (*pareve*) or butter (dairy)
❊ 4 carrots, thinly sliced
❊ 4 leeks, white part only, thinly sliced
❊ 2 potatoes, thinly sliced
❊ 1 cup chicken stock (or vegetarian stock, if dairy)
❊ 1 chicken bouillon cube (or vegetarian cube, if dairy)
❊ Salt and pepper, to taste

Quantity of carrots, leeks, and potatoes can be played with to find the exact taste desired.
For Pareve: *use margarine, vegetarian stock, and vegetarian bouillon.*
For Meat: *use margarine, chicken stock, and chicken bouillon.*
For Dairy: *use butter, vegetarian stock, and vegetarian bouillon.*

Recipe Instructions

❊ Melt a half stick of margarine in a large saucepan; add carrots and leeks. Cover and steam for 10 minutes.
❊ Add potatoes and one cup chicken stock.
❊ Cook covered until potatoes are soft, about half hour.
❊ Blend all ingredients with blender and return to pot (or use a hand-held blender in soup pot).
❊ Add chicken-flavored bouillon cube. Add salt and pepper, to taste.
❊ If too thick, add water.

Vegetable Soup

Vegetable Soup

Makes: 6 to 8 servings
Source: Mia

Ingredients

Fresh or frozen vegetables:

* 10 ounces mixed vegetables (found in freezer section)
* 16 ounces cut carrots
* 16 ounces small whole onions (or chopped)
* 16 ounces cut green beans

Other:

* 2 cut up stalks celery
* 1 bag chopped cabbage
* 2 46-ounce cans tomato juice
* 2 cut-up zucchini
* 2 veggie bouillon cubes
* 6 to 8 cups water
* 1 teaspoon crushed garlic
* Salt, pepper or lemon pepper to taste
* Parmesan cheese (optional)

Can freeze portions for future use. This is a low-calorie, high-nutrient soup. Adding Parmesan cheese makes the recipe dairy.

Recipe Instructions

* Put everything except Parmesan cheese together in stock pot.
* Bring to boil.
* Let simmer with lid on for 45 minutes.
* Serve hot.
* Sprinkle with Parmesan cheese (optional).

Soups ❊ 119

Easy Matzo Ball Soup

Makes: 8 to 10 servings
Source: Mia

Ingredients

❖ 1 box *matzo* ball soup mix with *matzo* ball mix
❖ Extra virgin olive oil
❖ 2 large carrots, peeled and sliced thin
❖ 2 stalks celery, chopped
❖ 1 large onion, chopped
❖ 1/2 to full bag thin soup noodles (depending upon desired amount of noodles)
❖ 1 teaspoon minced garlic
❖ 2 large baked chicken breasts, shredded (use meat only, no bones)
❖ Salt and pepper, to taste

For **Pareve**: *eliminate chicken and use* pareve *chicken broth.*
For **KP**: *use KP noodles or omit noodles.*

Recipe Instructions

❖ Follow directions on box to prepare *matzo* balls, only be sure to double the amount of oil called for on the box (this is what ensures that the *matzo* balls will be fluffy).
❖ Follow directions on box of *matzo* ball soup mix to bring water and soup mix to boil.
❖ When water with soup mix is boiling, add carrots, onions, celery, garlic, salt and pepper, to taste.
❖ Add *matzo* balls and cook as instructed on box.
❖ 10 minutes into cooking *matzo* balls, add shredded chicken breast and thin noodles, and cook for an additional 10 to 15 minutes.
❖ Adjust seasonings, to taste.

Matzo Ball Soup

Chicken Soup to Heal Your Soul

Makes: 6 to 8 servings
Source: Mom

Ingredients

✢ 1 large whole chicken, baked with seasoning or without
✢ 3 sticks celery, cut into 8 pieces
✢ 1 large onion, diced
✢ 2 carrots
✢ 2 bay leaves
✢ 1 tablespoon peppercorns
✢ 5 whole cloves
✢ 3 to 4 garlic cloves, sliced

Just the aroma of this soup cooking is enough to entice the senses and relax the body. The soup can be eaten right when cooked or can be saved and frozen for stock in other recipes.

Recipe Instructions

✢ After baking chicken, remove all meat and skin. Set skin aside for soup. Break meat into small pieces and freeze in air-tight bag.
✢ Take carcass of chicken and break into a handful of large pieces and place in large stock pot.
✢ Add skin of chicken and all remaining ingredients to pot, except cooked meat, and cover with cold water. Simmer slowly for two hours.
✢ Strain and discard bones, vegetables and spices.
✢ Cool stock and put in refrigerator overnight.
✢ The following day, skim fat from top of soup and discard.
✢ When ready to heat and serve, place pot over low heat.
✢ Add frozen chicken meat to soup as well as any other desired ingredients such as: fine noodles (during *Pesach*, add KP noodles), baby carrots, chopped onion, celery pieces, etc.
✢ Heat to desired temperature and adjust seasoning to taste.

Salads & Dips

"Eat greens in peace, not meat in peril!"

Shmuel HaNavi, Samuel the Prophet

Terrific Oriental Salad

Makes: 8 to 10 servings
Source: Karen Schott

Ingredients

* 2 to 2-1/2 heads iceberg lettuce, washed, or 4 regular bags of pre-cut lettuce
* 8 green onions sliced (whites only)
* 6 ounces sunflower seeds
* 6 ounces slivered almonds
* 6 ounces rice noodles (crispy in can)
* 1 11-ounce can mandarin oranges, drained

Dressing:
Make several hours before serving and let sit, sealed, at room temperature. Shake well before serving.

* 1 cup canola oil
* 1 cup seasoned rice vinegar
* 8 tablespoons brown sugar or brown sugar substitute equivalent

Recipe Instructions

* Place cleaned and drained lettuce in large bowl, add onions, sunflower seeds and almonds; toss together.
* Add dressing just before serving and toss well.
* Add rice noodles and toss again.
* Top with mandarin oranges.

Absolutely addictive. You have been warned.

Marinated Salads

Three-Bean Salad

Makes: 8 to 10 servings
Source: Mom

Ingredients

❖ 1 1-pound can red kidney beans, drained and rinsed
❖ 1 1-pound can wax beans, drained
❖ 1 1-pound can cut green beans, drained
❖ 1 large red onion, sliced lengthwise and cut thin
❖ 1 large red or green pepper, sliced

Dressing:
❖ 1/2 cup canola oil
❖ 1/2 cup cider vinegar
❖ 1 teaspoon salt
❖ 1/2 teaspoon white pepper

Recipe Instructions

❖ Place all veggies in large bowl.
❖ Mix dressing ingredients together and pour over veggies.
❖ Marinate overnight and serve with slotted spoon.

Sweet and Sour Cucumbers

Makes: 8 to 10 servings
Source: Doris Bjorklund

Ingredients

❖ 2 large imported cucumbers, thinly sliced. (If using regular cucumbers, cut in half and remove seeds with spoon.)

Dressing:
❖ 1 cup water
❖ 3/4 cup vinegar
❖ 3/4 cup sugar OR 8 packets of sugar substitute

Recipe Instructions

❖ Slice and soak cucumbers in salt water for at least 30 minutes. (Add salt water until water looks cloudy, stir and let dissolve.)
❖ Rinse and squeeze water out of cucumbers.
❖ Mix together dressing ingredients and stir until dissolved.
❖ Add cucumbers to dressing and refrigerate overnight.

Simple Egg Salad

Shabbat Table Salads

Simple Egg Salad

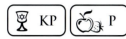

Makes: 4 to 6 servings
Source: Mia

Ingredients

✤ 8 hard boiled eggs, peeled and sliced both ways with slicer
✤ 1/2 cup chopped celery
✤ 1 tablespoon minced onion
✤ 3 heaping tablespoons mayonnaise
✤ Salt and black pepper to taste

Recipe Instructions

✤ Mix all ingredients together and serve chilled.

Spicy Egg Salad

Makes: 4 to 6 servings
Source: CD Kitchen

Ingredients

✤ 8 hard boiled eggs, peeled and sliced or mashed
✤ 1 tablespoon mayonnaise
✤ 1 tablespoon Dijon-style mustard
✤ 1 tablespoon spicy brown mustard
✤ 1 teaspoon paprika
✤ 1/2 medium yellow onion, minced
✤ Salt and black pepper, to taste

Recipe Instructions

✤ Combine all ingredients except the onion, salt, and pepper in a large bowl and mix well.
✤ Stir in onion, taste, then season with salt and pepper to taste.
✤ Serve chilled.

Matbucha

Makes: 6 to 8 servings
Source: Sarah Tikva Bell Almogue

Ingredients

* 3 cans diced tomatoes or 4 fresh tomatoes, chopped
* 1 to 3 chopped jalapeño peppers, to taste
* 20 or more chopped garlic cloves
* 3 tablespoons olive oil
* 1/8 to 1/4 cup sweet paprika, to taste

Recipe Instructions

* Chop the garlic and jalapeño, sauté with olive oil for one minute.
* Add paprika to mixture, sauté for one more minute.
* Add tomatoes and stir.
* Cook on medium-low flame for two to three hours stirring occasionally to avoid burning, should be a thick paste by end.
* Refrigerate for one to two hours before serving, overnight is best.

Simple Corn Salad

Makes: 4 to 6 servings
Source: Mia

Ingredients

* 1 can sweet corn, drained
* 3 heaping tablespoons mayonnaise
* 2 or 3 large pickles (sweet or sour as desired), chopped
* 1 small red pepper, chopped
* Salt and black pepper, to taste

Recipe Instructions

* Combine all ingredients in medium bowl and season with salt and pepper, to taste.
* Serve chilled and stir just prior to serving.

> *Sarah Tikvah makes the best version of the Middle Eastern dish, Matbucha, that I have ever had. As an aside, she met her husband, Avi, at our* Shabbat *dinner table so I feel particularly honored to include her in this book.* Mazal tov *Sarah and Avi!*

Summer Potato Salad

Makes: 6 quarts
Source: Karen Koreba

Ingredients

✥ 5 pounds red potatoes, boiled
✥ 1 dozen eggs, hard boiled
✥ 3 heaping tablespoons pickle relish
✥ 32 ounces light mayonnaise
✥ 1 heaping tablespoon yellow mustard
✥ 2-1/4 teaspoons salt
✥ 1/4 teaspoon black pepper
✥ 1 large onion, chopped

Recipe Instructions

✥ Cool potatoes and eggs after boiling, peel and slice all into large mixing bowl.
✥ In a small bowl, combine remaining ingredients and mix well.
✥ Pour mixture over potatoes and eggs, mix well and chill for several hours or overnight.
✥ Serve chilled.

One of my mom's best friends, Karen, would make this recipe on long summer days that would end with hamburgers on the grill and this potato salad. It was always one of my favorites growing up and still is today. Unfortunately Karen has since passed away, but our love for her and her memory lives on.

Avocado Dips

Simple Guacamole

Makes: 4 to 6 servings
Source: Hank from grad-school

Ingredients

* 2 plum tomatoes, chopped
* 5 to 6 scallions, chopped
* 2 avocados, pitted, peeled and mashed with fork
* 1 pinch chipotle chili pepper
* 1/2 lime

Recipe Instructions

* Mix the first four ingredients together in medium bowl.
* Squeeze half of one lime on top of mixture and stir before serving.

Kamoosh

Makes: 4 to 6 servings
Source: Mom

Ingredients

* 2 avocados, pitted, peeled and mashed with fork
* 1 tablespoon minced onions (dried)
* 1 tablespoon lemon juice
* 1 teaspoon salt
* 1/4 teaspoon chili powder
* 1 cup light mayonnaise

Recipe Instructions

* Stir onion, lemon juice, salt, and chili powder into mashed avocados in medium bowl that has a lid.
* Spread mayonnaise over top of mixture, sealing to the edge of the bowl, cover and chill several hours or overnight.
* When ready to serve, blend mixture together and serve with tortilla chips.

Optional

* Spread half teaspoon onto each chip, top with grated cheese and heat in 350 degree oven until cheese melts, about five to 10 minutes.
* Can also heat in microwave for one minute.

Simple Guacamole

Party Favorites

Hummus

Makes: 1 quart
Source: Marty Gurvey

Ingredients

* 4 cups (2-1/2 cans) garbanzo beans (chickpeas), drained
* 1/2 cup tahini (sesame paste)
* 1/3 cup warm water
* 1/3 cup extra-virgin olive oil
* Juice from 3 large lemons
* 4 to 6 large garlic cloves
* 1-1/2 teaspoons salt
* 2 teaspoons ground cumin seed
* Fresh ground pepper, to taste

Recipe Instructions

* Combine chickpeas, tahini, warm water, olive oil and lemon juice in bowl of food processor.
* With a steel blade, process until smooth and creamy, pausing to scrape down sides of bowl with spatula.
* Add garlic, salt, cumin seed and pepper to taste and process to blend; taste and correct seasoning if necessary.
* Store in covered container in fridge until ready to use.

Artichoke Spread

Makes: 4 servings
Source: Mom

Ingredients

* 1 cup light mayonnaise
* 1 cup Parmesan cheese
* 2 tablespoons dried onion
* 1 14-ounce can artichoke hearts, drained
* 1/2 teaspoon garlic powder

Recipe Instructions

* In food processor, blend artichoke hearts and run until chopped; add all other ingredients and blend until smooth.
* Bake in glass bowl at 350 degrees for 45 minutes.
* Serve with cocktail ryes.

Salads & Dips

"A cheerful heart is an unending banquet."

Proverbs, *Mishle*, 15:16

Meatless Lasagna

Makes: 6 to 8 servings
Source: Mom

Ingredients

* 10 ounces lasagna noodles, either cooked 5 minutes in boiling water OR oven-ready noodles
* 48 ounces meatless marinara sauce
* 3 packages sliced mozzarella cheese

Cheese filling:
* 24 to 30 ounces dry, unsalted farmer's cheese
* 8 ounces shredded Parmesan cheese
* 2 heaping tablespoons dried parsley flakes
* 2 eggs, well beaten
* 1/4 teaspoon white pepper

May be assembled earlier in the day and refrigerated until desired baking time. In this case must be baked for an additional 15 minutes before removing from oven. Leftovers freeze well.

Recipe Instructions

* Preheat oven to 375 degrees (electric oven, 325 degrees).

Prepare cheese filling:
* Crumble farmer's cheese into large bowl.
* Add all other cheese filling ingredients and mix until blended well.

Assemble lasagna in 9 x 13-inch glass or pyrex pan:
* Place a small amount of marinara sauce on bottom of pan to coat.
* Layer as follows, twice:
  * layer of noodles
  * layer half of cheese filling
  * layer half of sauce
  * layer of sliced cheese, overlapping slightly

* Bake for 30 minutes or until top starts to brown.
* Take out of oven and let stand for 15 minutes before serving. This is important so dish will slice and serve properly.

One of our favorite Shavuot meals, this lasagna recipe is mouth-watering. It is light yet filling and has a unique blend of flavors. Make note that as the recipe says, it really is important to allow the dish to rest prior to slicing or else it does not have time to solidify enough to cut properly.

Thin-Crust Pizza with Mushrooms and Olives

Traditional Thin-Crust Pizza

Makes: Two 12-inch pizzas
Source: Mia

Ingredients

❖ 1 package (2-1/4 teaspoons) active dry yeast
❖ 1-1/3 cups warm water
❖ 3-1/2 to 3-3/4 cups all-purpose flour
❖ 2 tablespoons cornmeal
❖ 2 tablespoons olive oil
❖ 1 tablespoon salt
❖ 1 tablespoon sugar
❖ 1 cup tomato sauce
❖ 1 to 2 large bags shredded mozzarella cheese
❖ Vegetables of choice, cut or chopped for toppings if desired

Recipe Instructions

To make dough:
❖ In large mixing bowl, dissolve yeast in warm water, add pinch of sugar and let stand for five minutes.
❖ Add remaining ingredients to bowl and mix by hand or with mixer for one minute until blended.
❖ Knead dough for about 10 minutes by hand or on low to medium speed with dough hook until dough is smooth and elastic.
❖ Transfer dough to lightly oiled bowl and turn over once to coat both sides with oil.
❖ Cover with lightweight towel or cloth and let rise until double in volume, approximately one to one and a half hours.
❖ Preheat oven to 475 degrees.
❖ Grease and dust two baking sheets with cornmeal.
❖ If using baking stone, place stone in oven and preheat for 45 minutes.
❖ Once risen, punch down dough and divide in half, roll each piece into a ball and let rest, loosely covered in plastic wrap for 10 to 15 minutes.
❖ Prepare desired toppings.
❖ Flatten each ball of dough one at a time on a lightly floured surface into 12-inch round, rolling and stretching dough.

Continued...

- Place each dough circle on prepared baking sheet.
- If using baking stone, dust with cornmeal prior to placing dough.
- Lift the edge of the dough and pinch to make crust and form lip.
- To prevent dough from getting soggy, brush top surface with olive oil and, with finger, push dents into surface of dough to prevent bubbling; let rest for 10 minutes.
- When pizza is ready to top: spread half cup tomato sauce across top of dough, followed by shredded cheese and any vegetable toppings desired.
- Bake on bottom rack of oven for about 12 minutes, until crust is browned and cheese is golden.
- Remove from the oven, slice, and serve at once.

> *Hand's down the best thin crust pizza I've eaten. And I'm not just saying that: when I make this pizza at parties people are constantly telling me I should open a pizza place. The fun part about making your own pizza is you can get as creative as you'd like with the toppings. It's also a fantastic activity to involve the kids with!*

Baked Noodles and Rice

Makes: 12 to 14 servings
Source: Mom

Ingredients

* 1/2 cup margarine
* 1/2 pound fine noodles
* 3 cups rice
* 2 packages onion soup mix
* 2 cans chicken soup
* 2 teaspoon soy sauce
* 1 can water
* 8 ounces water chestnuts, drained and chopped

Can be assembled earlier in the day and baked before dinner.
For Pareve*: use margarine and pareve chicken soup.*
For Meat*: use margarine and chicken soup.*
For Dairy*: use butter and pareve chicken soup.*

Recipe Instructions

* Preheat oven to 350 degrees.
* On stove top, melt margarine in large saucepan and brown fine noodles until golden.
* Add remaining ingredients and turn into three-quart casserole dish.
* Bake 45 minutes, uncovered.

Orange Noodle Pudding

Makes: 12 servings
Source: Grandma Terri Schaffner

Ingredients

❉ 2 8-ounce packages flat egg noodles, cooked and drained
❉ 1 cup sugar
❉ 1 pint sour cream
❉ Grated rind of 1 orange OR 1/4 teaspoon dried rind
❉ 1 cup cottage cheese (small curd)
❉ 1/4 pound melted butter
❉ 2 teaspoons vanilla
❉ 1 cup orange juice
❉ 6 egg yolks and 6 egg whites, separated
❉ 2 teaspoons salt
❉ 1/2 cup orange marmalade

Recipe Instructions

❉ Preheat oven to 350 degrees.
❉ Mix noodles, sugar, sour cream, orange rind, cottage cheese, butter, vanilla, orange juice, egg yolks, and salt in large bowl.
❉ Beat egg whites until stiff and fold into pudding mixture by hand.
❉ Pour into greased 12 x 14 x 2-inch casserole, filling to one half inch from top.
❉ Bake 45 minutes until firm; remove from oven.
❉ Spread half cup marmalade over top
and bake for 15 minutes until set and lightly brown.
❉ Serve with sour cream and brown sugar.

Orange Noodle Pudding

Desserts

"There's nothing wrong with a little--or a lot--of chocolate!"

Bubby Sara

Cookie Cheesecake

Makes: 1 pie-size cake
Source: Mia

Ingredients

❖ 2 8-ounce containers of whipped cream cheese
❖ 1/2 cup sour cream
❖ 1/2 cup sugar
❖ 1 teaspoon vanilla
❖ 3 tablespoons flour
❖ 1 tablespoon fresh lemon juice
❖ 3 eggs
❖ 1 8-ounce package chocolate sandwich cookies, crumbled and separated in half
❖ 1 pre-made graham cracker pie crust

Recipe Instructions

❖ Preheat oven to 350 degrees.
❖ Crumble sandwich cookies by placing in large Ziplock freezer bag and smashing cookies into coarse crumbs.
❖ In a large bowl, mix ingredients: Add to bowl in the order listed, adding only half of cookies and excluding pie crust.
❖ Pour mixture into pie crust and sprinkle remaining cookies over top of mixture.
❖ Bake for 30 to 40 minutes, until firm.
❖ Remove from oven and allow to cool completely before serving or, once cooled, cover with foil and store in refrigerator.

Cookie Cheesecake

Oma's Crescent Moon Cookies

Oma's Crescent Moon Cookies

 D

Makes: 30 cookies
Source: Oma

Ingredients

- 1 cup butter, room temperature
- 2/3 cup sugar
- 1 teaspoon pure vanilla extract
- 1 teaspoon almond extract
- 2-1/2 cups flour
- 1 cup ground almonds
- 1/4 cup sifted powdered sugar

Recipe Instructions

- Preheat oven to 350 degrees.
- Cream butter and sugar together until light and fluffy, add extracts and mix.
- Add flour and almonds, mix thoroughly.
- Take generous tablespoons of dough and roll each into a ball, about one inch in diameter, and then shape into crescents.
- Place onto parchment-lined baking sheet and bake for 15 to 20 minutes until light-golden-brown.
- Cool cookies on wire racks and dust with powdered sugar.

So many memories of sitting in my Oma's kitchen in her (at the time) fashionable green plastic chairs and rolling cookie dough on the white and green speckled table. She was always so patient as my sister and I played with the dough and made all sorts of shapes. Oma made so many wonderful and delicious cakes and dishes, but these cookies stand out among my favorites. The vanilla-almond scent is so inviting as they bake.

The Best Pareve Brownies

Makes: 15 to 20 brownies
Source: Betsy Forester

Ingredients

✣ 1 cup flour
✣ 1-1/2 cups sugar
✣ 2 sticks margarine
✣ 4 squares unsweetened baker's chocolate (*pareve*)
✣ 4 eggs
✣ 2 teaspoons vanilla
✣ dash of salt
✣ 1/2 bag of *pareve* chocolate chips (6 to 7 ounces)
✣ 3/4 cup nuts (optional)

Recipe Instructions

✣ Preheat oven to 350 degrees.
✣ Melt margarine with baker's chocolate in saucepan.
✣ In large bowl, beat together eggs, sugar, and vanilla.
✣ Slowly add flour and salt to bowl and mix with electric mixer.
✣ Continue mixing and add melted margarine and chocolate to bowl.
✣ Add chocolate chips and nuts to bowl and mix on low until blended.
✣ Pour into greased 11 x 13-inch pan and bake 25 to 30 minutes (check center with toothpick if desired to see if baked through).
✣ Slice when cooled.

The Best Pareve Brownies

Luscious Lemon Squares

Luscious Lemon Squares

Makes: 15 to 20 squares
Source: Karen Waldman

Ingredients

Crust:
* 3/4 cup unsalted margarine
* 1/3 cup powdered sugar
* 1-1/2 cups flour

Filling:
* 3 eggs
* 1-1/2 cups sugar
* 3 tablespoons flour
* 1/3 cup lemon juice

Garnish:
* Lemon zest

Recipe Instructions

Crust:
* Preheat oven to 350 degrees.
* Grease 9 x 13 inch glass dish.
* Cream margarine, powdered sugar, and flour in mixer and press into glass pan.
* Bake for 20 to 25 minutes.

Filling:
* Beat eggs until fluffy, slowly add sugar, flour, and lemon juice.
* Pour onto crust and bake for 20 to 25 minutes more.
* Cool and refrigerate to congeal.
* Before slicing to serve, sprinkle top with powdered sugar and garnish with lemon zest.

If there is such a thing as "professional grade lemon squares" then these are the real deal. It is hard to eat only one or two so be sure to make plenty. These also freeze very well so they can be made in advance and thawed right before use.

Baklava

Makes: 20 servings
Source: Neon Willie

Ingredients

* 1 16-ounce package phyllo dough
* 1 pound chopped nuts
* 1 cup butter or margarine
* 1 teaspoon ground cinnamon
* 1 cup water
* 1 cup sugar
* 1 teaspoon vanilla extract
* 1/2 cup honey

For Dairy: use butter.
For Pareve: use margarine and be certain phyllo dough is also pareve.

Recipe Instructions

* Preheat oven to 350 degrees.
* Butter bottom and sides of a 9 x 13-inch pan.
* In a bowl, toss nuts with cinnamon, set aside.
* Unroll phyllo dough; cut whole stack in half to fit pan.
* Cover dough with damp cloth to keep from drying out as you work.
* Place two sheets of dough in pan; butter thoroughly.
* Sprinkle two to three tablespoons of nut mixture on top.
* Continue layering dough and mixture until you've reached eight layers.
* Top with six to eight sheets of dough.
* Using sharp knife, cut into diamond or square shapes, then bake for about 50 minutes until golden and crisp.
* Make sauce while baklava is baking: boil sugar and water until sugar is melted, add vanilla and honey. Simmer for 20 minutes, stir to avoid burning.
* Remove baklava from oven and immediately spoon sauce over it. Let cool.
* Serve in cupcake wrappers and leave uncovered as it gets soggy if wrapped.

Baklava

Toffee Squares

Makes: 4 to 5 dozen
Source: Mom

Ingredients

✻ Approximately 1 package honey graham crackers (exact amount used will be determined by pan size)
✻ 2 sticks unsalted margarine (not frozen)
✻ 1 cup brown sugar
✻ 2-1/4 ounces of chopped nuts (almonds, pecans or walnuts)

Lining a pan with parchment paper prior to placing graham crackers will help prevent sticking.

Recipe Instructions

✻ Preheat oven to 375 degrees.
✻ Break graham crackers into quarters and line a jelly roll pan with pieces (use a pan with a lip).
✻ In saucepan, carmelize two sticks of margarine and one cup brown sugar. (Melt margarine and sugar over low flame, bring to boil and simmer for four to five minutes, stir occasionally to avoid burning. Mixture will bubble.)
✻ Pour mixture over graham crackers and spread evenly over top.
✻ Sprinkle with nuts and bake for 10 minutes.
✻ Let cool and lift cookies from pan, breaking into pieces.

Sesame Halava

Makes: 6 to 8 servings
Source: Saad Fayed

Ingredients

✣ 3 cups sesame seeds
✣ 3/4 cup tahini
✣ 1/2 cup sugar
✣ 1/2 cup honey
✣ 1/4 teaspoon cinnamon
✣ 1/4 teaspoon allspice

Recipe Instructions

✣ In skillet, heat sesame seeds over medium heat until lightly toasted.
✣ Once cooled, add sesame seeds to a food processor one cup at a time and blend.
✣ Add to food processor tahini, sugar, honey, cinnamon, and allspice, pulse until mixture is thick and nearly solid.
✣ Line baking pan with parchment paper or plastic wrap and press mixture evenly into pan.
✣ Cover and refrigerate until firm; cut into squares and serve.

Adler Family Cheesecake

Adler Family Cheesecake

Makes: 6 to 8 servings
Source: Mom

Ingredients

Crust:
* 1/2 stick butter or margarine
* 1 teaspoon cinnamon
* 3 tablespoons sugar
* 1-1/4 cups graham cracker crumbs

Filling:
* 3 8-ounce packages cream cheese, room temperature
* 1 cup sugar
* 1 tablespoon lemon juice
* 1 teaspoon vanilla
* 4 eggs, room temperature
* 1/8 teaspoon salt

Topping:
* 1 pint sour cream
* 1/3 cup sugar
* 1 teaspoon vanilla
* 1/8 teaspoon salt
* Fresh fruit (berries of choice) (optional)

Recipe Instructions
* Preheat oven to 350 degrees.

To prepare crust:
* Melt butter and in a bowl mix with cinnamon, crumbs, and sugar, blend with fork.
* Press mixture firmly into bottom and sides of spring form pan.
* Bake for eight minutes, remove from oven and let cool.

Assemble cake:
* In large bowl, combine cream cheese, sugar, and vanilla and mix on medium speed with electric mixer.
* Add lemon juice and salt to bowl, mix.
* Add one egg at a time to bowl, beating until well blended after each egg.
* Turn mixture into crumb lined pan and bake for 35 minutes or until firm.
* Let cake cool in oven after turning off heat, leaving oven door slightly open for heat to escape.
* Remove when cool and continue with topping.
* Preheat oven to 450 degrees.

Topping:
* Mix first four topping ingredients in bowl and pour over cooled cake.
* Bake for five minutes (no longer), remove and let stand to cool.
* Refrigerate until cold.
* Garnish with fruit on top if desired.

Desserts

Turtle Bars

Makes: 15 to 20 squares
Source: Nina Deitch

Ingredients

* 2 cups flour
* 1 cup packed light brown sugar
* 1/2 cup unsalted butter or margarine
* 1-1/2 cups pecan halves

Topping:
* 1/2 cup light brown sugar
* 2/3 cup unsalted butter or margarine
* 1 bag (11.5 ounces) chocolate chips

For **Pareve**: *use margarine and* pareve *chocolate chips.*
For **Dairy**: *use butter and milk chocolate chips.*

Recipe Instructions

* Preheat oven to 350 degrees.
* Mix flour, one cup sugar, and half cup butter or margarine until mixture resembles coarse crumbs.
* Press into ungreased 9 x 13-inch baking pan.
* Sprinkle pecans evenly over top.

Topping:
* Cook half cup sugar and two thirds cup butter or margarine in a small saucepan, stirring constantly until mixture begins to boil. Boil one minute, and then pour over pecans.
* Bake 20 to 25 minutes until firm.
* Remove from oven and immediately sprinkle chocolate chips over baked mixture. As it melts, spread to cover.
* Cool completely on wire rack, and then cut into squares.

Coffee and...

Banana Cake

Makes: 8 to 10 servings
Source: Liz Smith

Ingredients

* 1 cup shortening
* 4 eggs
* 2 cups sugar
* 2-1/2 teaspoons baking powder
* 2 cups flour
* 1 teaspoon salt
* 1-1/4 teaspoons baking soda
* 1 teaspoon vanilla extract
* 1 teaspoon banana or almond extract
* 1 cup chopped pecans
* 4 large very ripe bananas, mashed

Recipe Instructions

* Preheat oven to 350 degrees.
* Cream sugar, shortening, and eggs in mixer for three minutes.
* Stop mixer; add everything except nuts and bananas, and mix on medium setting until smooth.
* Add bananas and nuts, mix.
* Pour into greased and floured bundt pan OR two loaf pans, half full.
* Bake for 45 to 60 minutes.
* Test center wtih toothpick until clean, let cool, remove from pans.

Pumpkin Bread

Makes: 8 to 10 servings
Source: Moriah Pre-School, Deerfield, IL

Ingredients

* 3-1/3 cups flour
* 2 teaspoons baking soda
* 1-1/2 teaspoons salt
* 1 teaspoon cinnamon
* 1 teaspoon nutmeg
* 3 cups sugar
* 1 cup vegetable oil
* 4 eggs
* 2/3 cup water
* 15-ounce can of solid packed pumpkin
* Splash of vanilla

Recipe Instructions

* Preheat oven to 350 degrees.
* Put all dry ingredients into a bowl.
* Make a center hole, and add wet ingredients.
* Mix well.
* Grease and flour a bundt pan or two loaf pans.
* Pour pumpkin mixture into pan(s), leaving half inch room at top of pan(s).
* Bake for one hour.
* Let cool; remove from pan(s).

Desserts ❋ **163**

Apple Crisp

Makes: 12 servings
Source: Betsy Forester

Ingredients

* 1/2 cup flour
* 1/2 cup sugar
* 1/2 cup firmly packed brown sugar
* 4 tablespoons chopped nuts (pecans, walnuts, or macadamia)
* 1/4 teaspoon cinnamon
* 5 tablespoons margarine or butter
* 10 cups peeled, thinly sliced apples of choice
* Cooking spray
* 6 tablespoons apricot preserves

For Dairy: use butter.
For Pareve: use margarine.

Recipe Instructions

* Preheat oven to 375 degrees.
* Combine first five ingredients in medium bowl.
* Cut in margarine until mixture resembles a coarse meal; set aside.
* Spray 11 x 13-inch baking pan with cooking spray.
* Line bottom of pan with apples.
* Drop apricot preserves by the teaspoonful onto apple slices, spread gently with spatula.
* Sprinkle crumb mixture evenly across top.
* Bake for 35 to 40 minutes or until bubbly and golden.
* Can serve warm with vanilla ice cream or even tastes good at room temperature or chilled.

Chocolate Covered Dates

Makes: 5 to 6 servings
Source: Saad Fayed

Ingredients

✣ 16 ounces semi-sweet *pareve* chocolate, chopped
✣ 20 to 25 pitted dates
✣ Toasted almonds, walnuts, or pistachios
✣ Coconut flakes
✣ Skewer and parchment paper

Recipe Instructions

✣ Line large baking sheet with parchment paper: you will place dipped dates onto this paper.
✣ Stuff each date with nut of your choice.
✣ Melt chocolate in microwave or over low heat, stirring halfway through cooking time.
✣ Using a skewer, dip each date into the chocolate; allow excess chocolate to fall away by carefully rotating the skewer.
✣ Place dipped date on parchment paper and sprinkle with coconut flakes.
✣ Allow dates to set in the refrigerator for about 20 to 30 minutes before serving.

Fun for Kids

Taffy Apples

Makes: 5 apples
Source: Stephanie Merkin

Ingredients

- 5 apples of choice
- 1 bag of caramels
- 5 wooden sticks
- 2 tablespoons water

Recipe Instructions

- Unwrap caramels and put them into medium saucepan.
- Add two tablespoons water.
- Melt caramels on very low flame in saucepan, stirring to prevent burning.
- Wash apples and put sticks into apple at core.
- Dip apples into caramel, and either eat or set on wax paper to cool.

Pareve Ice Cream

Makes: 4 to 6 servings
Source: Bubby

Ingredients

- 1 container Rich's Whip™ or equivalent non-dairy whipped topping
- 2 eggs, separated
- 1 teaspoon vanilla
- 2 tablespoons cocoa or instant coffee
- 1/2 cup sugar

Recipe Instructions

- With electric mixer, beat whole container of Rich's Whip (or other *pareve* whipped topping) until stiff, eight to 10 minutes.
- Add two egg yolks, vanilla, and cocoa or coffee and beat until well blended.
- In separate bowl, beat egg whites and sugar into stiff meringue, fold together with other mixture.
- Pour into serving bowl, mold, or nine-inch square pan and freeze overnight.

Desserts ✽ **167**

Chocolate Peanut Butter Diamonds

Makes: 12 to 15 servings
Source: Sharon Partush

Absolutely addictive, cannot keep them in the house or will be eaten by me. I only make these when I know I have a big crowd so that none will be left over!

Ingredients

✣ 4 sticks margarine (or butter for dairy)
✣ 4 cups powdered sugar
✣ 1 18-ounce jar creamy peanut butter
✣ 1-1/2 cups graham cracker crumbs
✣ 1-1/4 cups *pareve* chocolate chips (or milk chocolate for dairy)

Recipe Instructions

✣ Line a jelly roll pan with parchment paper.
✣ In medium saucepan over low heat, melt two sticks of margarine.
✣ Remove from heat and add sugar, peanut butter, and graham cracker crumbs; stir to combine.
✣ Spread mixture onto pan. Place piece of wax paper or parchment paper over peanut butter, and use a kid-sized rolling pin or palm of hand to pat evenly into the pan.
✣ In a small saucepan over low heat, melt the remaining two sticks of margarine and chocolate chips together, stir to combine, then pour over the peanut butter layer.
✣ While chocolate mixture is still hot, tilt pan to spread thick, even layer that coats peanut butter. Take care not to manipulate chocolate too much.
✣ Refrigerate for half hour, and then cut into diamond-shaped pieces.

Shabbat & Chaggim

"Let all who are hungry come and eat."

The *Pesach Haggadah*

A Word About This Section

Shabbat and the holidays are some of the most beautiful, meaningful, and rewarding times in Jewish life. Each of us has grown up with our own stories, traditions, and cultures that bring value to the home and the table. If, for some reason, you did not grow up with these elements, then you are given the gift of being able to create your own customs and traditions for you and your family. Regardless of how you choose to celebrate, each of these holy days carries great opportunity and significance. For Shaul and me, and our family dynamics, we have had to find ways to blend Ashkenazi and Sepharadi traditions and practices to create experiences that meet all needs. To me this is a blessing and has caused me to open my eyes and my heart to the variety of sacred ways people can connect with, and relate to G-d.

There are hundreds of books written about the various Jewish holidays that go into depth about the meanings and various ways to observe the holidays, depending upon your culture (observance level) and personal preference. My goal in sharing these "bite-size" briefs about the holidays is to give you a taste of what each is about, to "whet your appetite," and entice you to "rise" to the occasion of each *chag*, both for yourself and your family.

The Jewish calendar, and the holidays contained within it, are designed as an intricate system to help us elevate ourselves if we so choose. The information I have provided cuts right to the core of the opportunities that each *chag* provides. I have shared some traditional recipes wrapped in the consciousness of the holiday and sprinkled with the key details necessary for a delicious and meaningful experience.

Chag Sameach! Happy Holidays!

Shabbat

Lichvod Shabbat Kodesh
To Honor the Holiness of the Sabbath

Shabbat is not simply a day of the week that we can use for rest and relaxation (although *Shabbat* naps are the best), but rather it is a day of such tremendous opportunity to draw closer to *HaShem*. The power of *HaShem*'s Light is revealed to us through the reading of the *Torah* portion, the three *seudot* (meals) that we are meant to partake in, words of an inspiring Rabbi, and the opportunity to stop daily activity and spend time with friends and family. According to *Kabbalah*, *Shabbat* is an opening in time designed by *HaShem* for us to gather spiritual strength to meet the demands of our lives with courage and *bitachon*. Those who observe the Sabbath are provided with an extra "boost" of energy to take into the new week.

Preparing for *Shabbat* requires thought and care in order to prepare all food prior to candle lighting time each week.

Setting a *Shabbat* Table

Traditions vary around the world for setting the *Shabbat* table; however, certain staples are most common. Here are the necessary "ingredients" for a traditional *Shabbat* table and meal:

❈ *Challah* (two minimum)
❈ Wine and/or grape juice
❈ Water (for *Kiddush*)
❈ Salt (for *challah*)
❈ *Natlan* (two-handled cup for ritual washing of hands prior to blessing the *challah*) and clean hand towel
❈ *Challah* cover, knife, and cutting board
❈ Salad plates and salad forks (for serving fish as first course with various salads)
❈ Dinner plates and clean forks (with knives and spoons for second course)
❈ Wine glasses and/or drinking cups
❈ Dinner napkins
❈ Fresh flowers in vase

Shabbat Prep "To Do" List

Based on my personal experience, if you didn't grow up in a *shomer Shabbat* home where the preparation for *Shabbat* becomes second nature, learning to prepare for *Shabbat* in this way can take practice and patience. Here are a few tips to speed the learning curve:

❖ Plan ahead: By Wednesday night, have an idea of what your menu will be and prepare your shopping list. Shop Thursday or Friday morning. Prepare items ahead if possible and refrigerate.
❖ Create a "*Shabbat* List" of things to do right before *Shabbat* that you can reference every week. For example: prepare lights in house, fill water heater and plug in, plug in warming plate, remove refrigerator light, prepare cholent, etc.
❖ Prepare *Shabbat* clothing for the family (dry cleaning, etc.) by Thursday, so you are not rushed on Friday.
❖ Friday is a great day to clean house. There is nothing like a clean and straightened home to welcome *Shabbat*!
❖ For an excellent and easy-to-use guide on warming food on *Shabbat* please read the slim volume of *Laws of Cooking on the Sabbath and Festivals* by Ehud Rosenberg.

Shabbat Dinner Menu Ideas

The *Shabbat* meal traditionally begins with *Kiddush* over the wine and "*HaMotzie*" over the *challah*. Other songs and blessings are included such as singing "*Shalom Aleichem*," "*Ashet Chayil*," blessing of the children and *Netilat Yadayim* before *HaMotzie*. Some also include various passages from the *Zohar* or other *Kabbalistic* texts. Consult a Rabbi or *siddur* for specific prayers that would be appropriate for your *Shabbat* celebration.

After *HaMotzie* is said and everyone has had a first bite of *challah*, the meal begins with a selection of salads (see section on salads for ideas) as well as some type of fish dish. A typical *Ashkenazi* meal will include gefilte fish with horseradish or some type of fish salad, while a traditional Sepharadi table will include some type of cooked fish, such as the Moroccan Fish, or perhaps baked salmon with some spice.

The main meal for both Ashkenazi or Sepharadi homes will typically include a dish with beef or chicken, some type of carbohydrate dish such as rice or potato, as well as a vegetable dish. There are a wide variety of choices as seen in the Meat, Poultry, Vegetable, and Pasta sections.

The final indulgence of the *Shabbat* meal will include a touch of sweetness in the form of a plate of cut-up fresh fruit, as well as one or two *pareve* desserts. There are many scrumptious ones to choose from in the dessert section!

When the meal has drawn to conclusion, the final prayer over the food is recited together: *Birkat HaMazon*. The prayer is extremely important, as it elevates the sparks of Light that have been encased in the food we have just eaten. *Shabbat shalom*!

The Month of Tishrei
An Opportunity for Re-Creation

Beginning with *Rosh Hashanah* and moving through *Yom Kippur*, *Sukkot*, *Shemini Atzeret*, and *Simchat Torah*, the entire month of *Tishrei* is designed as a window of time for us to continually reflect on who we have been and who we wish to become. It is a time for us to communicate personally with G-d, intimately accounting for our actions and thoughts during the prior year and discerning how we wish to reach new levels of growth and spiritual maturity in the coming year. Again, and again, we are given the chance to ask for, and to give, forgiveness, and to make *tshuva* or *tikkunim* (corrections) for our prior choices and actions.

Throughout this time we are mandated to participate in several meals, including blessings over wine, bread, and a variety of foods. We are given the opportunity to connect with the divine energy of each holiday through the partaking of ceremonial foods (or, on *Yom Kippur*, the abstaining from those foods) for one purpose only: to cleanse and elevate our *neshama* in order to truly become a better version of ourselves.

Both the spiritual and physical work of this month are very demanding and require thoughtful intention. Use the time of preparing meals during this month as a means for reflection and as an opportunity to share with those whom you love, as well as those who are less fortunate than you.

During this month, it is customary to serve *challot* that are round in shape, instead of braided and long, signaling a time for renewal, symbolizing the life cycle of which we are all a part.

Rosh Hashanah
The Physical New Year and Creation of Adam

Rosh Hashanah is actually understood to be the physical creation and birthday of *Adam HaRishon*, *HaShem's* first human creation from whom all human beings stem. Our connection on this day is to the root source of our very existence, and with proper intention in our prayers, we can tap into and re-create who we are at the core of our beings. *Rosh Hashanah* is a time for meaningful self-reflection. It is the start of a 10-day period during which we can turn back time in our minds and review that which we have done, both positive and negative. It is the start of a powerful month, giving us one opportunity after the other to actually change our lives through *cheshbon nefesh*, literally translated as "calculations of the soul." Beginning on this holiday we are divinely mandated to review our past year with a constructively critical eye, identifying those actions and thoughts we could have done better and opening the gateway for forgiveness and profound change. It is with this consciousness that we begin each and every Jewish new year.

The *Rosh Hashanah Seder*

Although the *Rosh Hashanah Seder* can be celebrated by Jews of all backgrounds, it originally comes from *Sepharadi* tradition and lineage, and is something quite meaningful and powerful. Rooted in mystical secrets of *Kabbalah*, the combinations of certain foods and their blessings at this pivital time of year are meant to create blessings and opportunitiy in the new year. Various communities have their own order in which they recite the blessings and eat the foods. Consult with your Rabbi to learn more about the practice of a *Rosh Hashanah Seder* or there are several online resources that detail the prayers and practices of a *Rosh Hashanah Seder*.

Items for *Rosh Hashanah Seder*

In addtion to preparing a large meal, which will include wine for *Kiddush* and at least two round *challot*, the following items are to be blessed and then eaten at the start of the meal:

✤ Dates
✤ Pomegranates
✤ Apples (often eaten with honey)
✤ String beans/rubia -fenugreek/carrots
✤ Pumpkin or gourd (*k'ra*)
✤ Spinach or beetroot leaves (*selek*)
✤ Leeks, chives, scallions, or cabbage (*karti*)
✤ Sheep's head or fish head (or head of lettuce for vegetarian option)

Shanah tovah u' metukah!
Have a good and sweet new year!

Rosh Hashanah

Yom Kippur
Reaching Greater Spiritual Heights

Yom Kippur is one of the holiest days of the year. It requires fasting from nightfall on the evening of *Yom Kippur* and the time of the *Kol Nidre* prayer, to the following day upon completion of the *Ne'ilah* prayer.

Why include a section about a fast day in a cookbook? There are two very important reasons: First is to understand why we do NOT eat and what this does for us spiritually, and second is to understand how to prepare for and then to break the fast itself.

As I have described earlier in this book, the act of eating food brings two worlds together: when food is eaten, the spiritual world of the *neshama* blends with the physical world of the body. On the holiest day of *Yom Kippur* when our spiritual connection to *HaShem* is meant to be the strongest and ultimate focus, and when we stand to be judged in *HaShem's* court, we deny the body physical sustenance so that the entire focus of our being is on the spiritual connection and reverence we have for *HaShem* and our *neshama*. By removing food, we force the body to allow the *neshama* to elevate a little higher, we tell the body that it is the *neshama* that is in charge today, and that for today we will not be a slave to the needs of the body.

Prior to the fast, it is tradition for some to eat five small meals throughout the day before the fast, taking care to recite both *HaMotzie* and *Birchat HaMazon* each time, in an effort to begin the process of elevating the *neshama* and preparing the body for lack of food and drink as the *neshama* reaches new heights. Breaking the fast is customarily done with light foods, which might include juices, fish, dairy dishes, fruits, breads, and so on, taking care not to overwhelm the body, which has just undergone deprivaton for a 25-hour period.

Those who wish to fulfill a great mitzvah make it a tradition to immediately begin construction of the *sukkah* for the holiday of *Sukkot* upon completion of the break-the-fast meal of *Yom Kippur*. *Tzom kal*, have an easy fast.

Sukkot

Sukkot
Accepting Abundance and Blessings

There are several items that are unique to the holiday of *Sukkot* that are needed to celebrate this festive holiday:
* *Lulav* and accompanying branches
* *Etrog*
* A *sukkah* sized according to need
* *Schach* for the top of the *sukkah*
* A *siddur* or *machzor* for *Sukkot* that provides all of the necessary prayers for the holiday, including the prayer for sitting in the *sukkah*

All of the above can usually be purchased through your synagogue, your local Judaica store, or online.

Other important items:
* Decorations for the interior of the *sukkah* (a terrific job for kids!)
* Table and chairs
* Inflatable mattress and/or sleeping bag
* Delicious food!!

Don't forget to make some round challot and to have plenty of wine and grape juice available for blessings and meals!

"LaShev BaSukkah"
"To sit in the *Sukkah*"

Sukkot is a holiday of harvesting, a time of great celebration and abundance, both physically and spiritually. According to *halacha*, during the eight days of *sukkot* a Jew is meant to eat every meal in the *sukkah* at the least, and men specifically are meant to sleep in the *sukkah* as well. The *sukkah* becomes our home and place of sustenance for the duration of the holiday. During this time we are meant to "harvest" all of the spiritual energy generated by us during the month of *Tishrei*. It is the time to reap the benefits of all of the hard spiritual and physical work done since *Rosh Hashanah*. It is a joyous time!

Quite like decorating our homes, it is tradition to decorate the inside of the *sukkah* as well to make it special, as this space is often shared with a long list of guests throughout the holiday. Significant items to decorate with might include: photos of loved ones past; photos of *tzadikkim*; harvest foods; art made by your kids, like paper chains and pictures of *sukkot*, or anything meaningful to the family.

Cooking for this holiday is always special and can include a large variety of dishes according to the family favorites.

The *sukkah* itself is not just any tent or make-shift dwelling. According to *Kabbalah* and *halacha*, the *sukkah* is actually a metaphysical portal that heaps blessings upon all Jewish souls who dwell within it. As such, the *sukkah* must be built with great care and must also meet very specific guidelines to be considered a "kosher dwelling" for the holiday. It is advisable to check with your Rabbi for details on what constitutes a kosher *sukkah* so that you may bring the greatest amount of blessings to your *sukkah* and to all those who enter it. *Chag sameach!*

Chanukah
Playing in the World of Miracles

The energy of *Chanukah* is powerful and illuminating. During *Chanukah*, we are each granted the unique opportunity to connect with, and bring into our own lives, the world of miracles–that which exists above the nature of things. By lighting the *chanukia* each of the eight nights of *Chanukah*, we welcome this Light into our homes and into our hearts, and open ourselves to possibilities that are beyond what we can imagine.

According to the sages, on *Chanukah* it is important to bask in the light of the candles and spend as much time absorbing this energy as possible. Dream your greatest dreams. Think about the tremendous miracles that occurred at this time hundreds of years ago, when the Maccabis were victorious against overwhelming odds and experienced the miracle of the oil burning for eight days, when it was only enough for one. Take the opportunity during *Chanukah* to shed the limitations set upon you by yourself and others, and open your heart to the notion that anything is truly possible.

Chanukah sameach! Nissim v'niflaot!
Happy *Chanukah*! Wishing you miracles and wonders!

Potato Latkes

Makes: 2 dozen latkes
Source: Shaul

Ingredients

* 5 large potatoes
* 2 large onions
* 1 cup parsley, chopped
* 1 tablespoon salt
* 1 tablespoon black pepper
* Grapeseed oil

Recipe Instructions

* Grate potatoes and onions into large bowl and mix well.
* Add parsley, salt, and pepper; mix well.
* In large skillet, cover bottom of pan with oil and heat on high until hot.
* Form latkes by hand, approximately three inches in diameter each, and place in oil.
* Allow to brown on first side and then carefully flip and brown second side.
* Once latkes are browned and cooked through, remove from oil and place on baking sheet or foil plan lined with paper towels to absorb excess oil.
* Serve warm with sour cream or apple sauce.

Shabbat & Chaggim ❋ 185

Chanukah Sufganiyot (Israeli Jelly Doughnuts)

Makes: 20 doughnuts
Source: Bubby

Ingredients

✤ 2 tablespoons active dry yeast
✤ 1/2 cup warm water
✤ 1/4 cup plus 1 teaspoon sugar, plus more for rolling
✤ 2-1/2 cups flour, plus more for dusting
✤ 2 large eggs
✤ 2 tablespoons unsalted margarine (or butter for dairy)
✤ 1/2 teaspoon salt
✤ 3 cups vegetable oil, plus more for bowl
✤ 1 cup seedless jam of choice, or cream-style filling (choose pareve filling for pareve recipe)

Recipe Instructions

✤ In a small bowl, combine yeast, warm water, and one teaspoon sugar; set aside until foamy (about 10 minutes).
✤ Place flour in a large bowl, make a well in the center and add eggs, yeast mixture, quarter cup sugar, margarine, nutmeg, and salt.
✤ On a well-floured surface, knead until dough is soft and smooth and bounces back when poked with a finger.
✤ Place in an oiled bowl, cover and allow to rise until doubled (about one to one and a half hours).
✤ On a lightly floured surface, roll dough to quarter-inch thickness.
✤ Using a 2-1/2-inch round cutter or drinking glass, cut twenty rounds, cover with plastic wrap, and let rise fifteen minutes.
✤ In medium saucepan over medium heat, heat oil until a deep-frying thermometer registers at 370 degrees.
✤ Using slotted spoon, carefully slip four dough rounds into oil; fry until golden, about 40 seconds.
✤ Turn doughnuts over; fry until golden on second side.
✤ Using a slotted spoon, transfer to paper-towel-lined baking sheet and roll in sugar while warm.
✤ Repeat frying and rolling until all doughnuts complete.
✤ Fill pastry bag with choice of filling; use #4 tip.
✤ Using wooden skewer or toothpick, make a hole in one side of each doughnut and then insert tip of pastry bag to fill doughnut.

Chanukah Sufganiyot

Tu B'Shvat

Tu B'Shvat
Connecting Heaven and Earth

Tu B'Shvat is traditionally known as the "holiday of the trees" or the "birthday of the trees." Children and adults alike love this holiday, and in modern times it has been connected to all things green and eco-friendly. These concepts are wonderful and endearing; however, *Tu B'Shvat* is a holiday of great depth and mystical power, literally connecting all of the worlds of the One Great Tree: The Tree of Life or *Etz HaChayim*. Through *Kabbalah*, we understand that *Tu B'Shvat* reveals the energy and Light of *HaShem* as it moves from the highest realms of the Tree of Life (*Keter* of *Atzilut*) down through the many levels of the tree to where we exist, in the *Malchut* of *Assiya* or earthly level, of The Tree. It is a day of celebrating all the bounty that *HaShem* provides through his awesome creation of nature. Traditionally, this day is celebrated with planting trees, visits to forests, special awareness of the gifts of nature, as well as with a special *Tu B'Shvat Seder* providing us with the opportunity to bless the variety of nature's gifts and to connect with tremendous Light.

The *Tu B'Shvat Seder*

There are many wonderful *seder* formats that are available online for the *Tu B'Shvat Seder*, and it is always recommended to consult with your rabbi to learn what celebrations might be happening in your community.

Items needed for a *Kabbalistic Tu B'Shvat Seder*:

✢ White wine
✢ Red wine
✢ Pomegranates, figs
✢ Walnuts, peanuts, almonds
✢ Olives, dates, cherries, plums, apricots
✢ Berries of varying kinds and grapes
✢ Fragrant spices and/or fruits that are particularly fragrant
✢ Something made of wheat (cookies, etc.)

It is important to pay close attention to exactly which blessings to say over each item of the *seder* and in what specific order to both drink the wine as well as eat the foods. *Chag sameach!*

Purim
Concealing in Order to Reveal

Seudat Purim: The Purim Feast

According to *Kabbalah*, the revelation of Light during *Purim* is even greater than that of *Yom Kippur*. How can it be that a holiday where we conceal ourselves in costume and drink alcohol until we are in great *simcha*, joy, can possibly hold greater potential than the holiest day of the year? Because anything received in *simcha* is automatically at a higher level than anything received in *yirah*, awe or fear such as what we experience on *Yom Kippur*. On *Purim*, we are commanded to be in *simcha*. We are obligated to reach a state of such great *simcha* "*Ad Shelo Yadah*," "until we do not know"–do not know what? Do not know the difference between Mordechai and Haman! In other words, we need to be in such a level of *simcha* and to reveal so much Light that we cannot tell the difference between the Light and the dark, because in such a state EVERYTHING IS LIGHT! EVERYTHING IS GOOD! EVERYTHING IS BLESSINGS, and the Light irradicates any darkness! On *Purim*, it is tradition to enjoy a great feast, to share by giving *mishloach manot* (gift baskets), and to give *tzedakah* to the poor. *Purim sameach!* Happy *Purim*!

Hamantaschen

Makes: 4 dozen cookies
Source: Chabad.org

These are the traditional Purim *three-cornered pastries filled with poppy seed or other sweet filling.*

Ingredients

❖ 1 cup sugar
❖ 1/3 cup oil
❖ 1/3 cup shortening
❖ 3 eggs
❖ 1/2 cup orange juice
❖ 4 cups flour
❖ 3 teaspoons baking powder
❖ 1 teaspoon salt
❖ 1 egg, beaten
❖ 2 pounds filling of choice (poppy seed, fruit jams or jellies, chocolate spread or chips, etc.)

Continued...

Hamantaschen

Recipe Instructions

✤ Preheat oven to 350 degrees.
✤ Cream sugar, oil and shortening; add eggs and juice and mix well.
✤ Blend with dry ingredients and roll dough into ball; divide dough into four parts.
✤ Roll out each piece of dough very thin (approximately one-eighth inch) on a floured surface.
✤ With the rim of a cup or glass (depending upon desired size), cut into the dough to make circles.
✤ Place a half to two-thirds teaspoon of filling in the middle of each circle.
✤ To shape triangle: lift up right and left sides, leaving the bottom side down, and bring both sides to meet at center above filling. Lift bottom side up to center to meet other two sides and pinch together.
✤ Brush pastries with beaten egg before baking; place on greased cookie sheet, and bake for approximately 20 minutes.

Pesach

Pesach
The Spiritual New Year & Time of Rebirth

Preparing for Renewal: Cleaning away "*chametz*," both physically and spiritually.

The month of *Nissan*, during which *Pesach* takes place, is actually the spiritual New Year. Everything that eventually manifests itself physically began somewhere in the spiritual realm. *Pesach* is the time for spiritual re-birth and cleansing. It is the start of spring-time and renewal. The mandated act of removing "*chametz*" from our homes and lives during the eight days of *Pesach* is symbolic for removing all of those things–mentally, physically and spiritually–that inhibit our growth. We are told during this time of year to get our proverbial acts together and kick the laziness out of the house and out of ourselves. Get up, grab a mop, be with your thoughts, and get cleaning, inside of yourself, as well as your surroundings. Don't forget the hidden corners of the mind and under the seat of the ego. The more physical cleaning we do directly impacts the depth of cleaning we are able to do internally. This is a unique opportunity that comes but once a year. Don't miss out.

The *Pesach Seder*: The most well-known of all the *seders*, the *Pesach Seder* is the ultimate adventure into the spiritual realm. Through a calculated series of preparations, foods, and prayers, we can literally create for ourselves new perspectives on life, new investments in personal growth, and new levels of spiritual existence within this world.

Items needed for *Pesach Seder*:

✤ *Shmurah Matzo*, several pieces per participant
✤ *Matzo* covers
✤ Wine and grape juice, four cups per participant
✤ Horseradish or Romaine lettuce for bitter herbs for *seder* plate and each participant
✤ *Haggadah* for every participant
✤ *Charoset* (see following recipes) for *seder* plate and participants
✤ Shankbone for *seder* plate
✤ Hard boiled eggs for *seder* plate and participants
✤ Vegetable for *Karpas* (potato, onion, celery, radish or parsley) for *seder* plate and participants

Shabbat & Chaggim ❋ 195

Ashkenazi and Sepharadi guidelines for the *Pesach Seder* vary by location, lineage, and customs. There are several key components that are part of both *seders*; however, choice of foods, ways to involve children in the *seder*, as well as various practical components, are diverse. Given the magnitude of the holiday of *Pesach*, it is wise to consult with your Rabbi to ensure that you are including all necessary components that are appropriate for your family.

Kashrut and Pesach

It is important to note that *Pesach* comes with several additional guidelines and laws when it comes to kashrut. *Please consult with your Rabbi for specific details as to how your customs and community observe* kashrut *during* Pesach. *Review each of the following recipes carefully to see if it fits within the guidelines given for your way of observance.* In general:

✤ All other laws of kashrut as discussed earlier in this book apply during *Pesach*.

✤ During *Pesach*, it is considered essential that nothing come in contact with you that might contain *chametz*. This includes all foods, drinks, and body care products such as soap, toothpaste, make-up, etc.

✤ Ashkenazi and Sepharadi practices of what foods are allowed differ. Please check with your Rabbi to know what allowances and restrictions apply to you.

✤ It is common practice to either *kasher* (to make kosher) dishes, pots, etc. specially for *Pesach* or to have a completely separate set of dishes, pots, etc. that are used only during *Pesach*.

✤ All appliances must be specially *kashered* for *Pesach* prior to cooking for *Pesach*, and the entire kitchen and home must be cleaned and rid of *chametz* (don't forget your cars, strollers, knapsacks, car seats, and all other fun places where a *chametz* loves to hide!).

✤ Cleaning for *Pesach* is serious business. Make a list of all that needs to be done and allow the necessary time prior to the start of the holiday. *Chag sameach v' kasher!* Have a happy and kosher *Pesach*!

Pesach Essentials

Ashkenazi-Style *Charoset*

Makes: Enough for 2 *seders*
Source: Mom

Ingredients

- 4 unpeeled apples, chopped
- 1 cup chopped pecans
- 2 teaspoons honey
- 1/2 teaspoon cinnamon
- 2 tablespoons Concord wine

Recipe Instructions

- Mix all ingredients together in medium bowl and chill until placing on table in smaller bowls.

Sepharadi-Style *Charoset*

Makes: Enough for 2 *seders*
Source: Shaul

Ingredients

- 2 jars Silan (honey of dates sold in a jar, usually a specialty item available around *Pesach*)
- 2 cups crushed walnuts

Recipe Instructions

- Mix all ingredients together in large bowl and chill until placing on table in smaller bowls.

Although both of these recipes for charoset *are excellent, the truth is over the years even my Ashkenazi kids prefer the Sepharadi-style dish. I still always make both to satisfy the diversity of our guests so that everyone can savor his or her own tradition.*

Popover Rolls

Makes: 24 to 36 rolls
Source: Dad (Okay, so really it's my mom's recipe, but my dad does make these every year!)

Ingredients

- 1 cup grapeseed, walnut, or olive oil
- 4 cups water
- 4 cups *matzo* meal
- 2 teaspoons salt
- 14 jumbo eggs or 18 large eggs

Recipe Instructions

- Preheat oven to 400 degrees (electric 375 degrees).
- In large pot bring oil and water to boil over high heat.
- Turn flame to medium and add salt and *matzo* meal.
- Stir over medium flame until dough pulls from sides.
- Turn off flame and cool for 15 minutes.
- Add a few eggs at a time, mixing until blended well.
- Heavily grease muffin tins, insides and top.
- Put heaping tablespoon of dough into each muffin, filling at least half way.
- Bake for 15 minutes at 400 degrees (electric 375 degrees), turn down to 375 degrees (electric 350 degrees) and bake 40 minutes. Check at 30 minutes.
- Done when golden brown.

Almond Chicken

Makes: 16 smaller pieces
Source: Mom

Ingredients

- 4 full or 8 half boneless, skinless chicken breasts, cut in half
- Grapeseed oil

Seasoned Starch:
- 1 teaspoon salt
- 1/4 teaspoon white pepper
- 1/3 cup potato starch

Egg Mixture:
- 2 eggs beaten with 1/8 cup water

Crumb mixture:
- 1 cup ground almonds
- 1 cup *matzo* meal
- 1/2 teaspoon garlic powder
- 1/2 teaspoon onion powder
- 1/4 teaspoon paprika

Recipe Instructions

- Preheat oven to 350 degrees.
- Wash and dry chicken breasts; cut each into two or three pieces.
- Dredge in seasoned starch mixture on both sides.
- Using tongs, dip into egg mixture and let drip off.

Continued...

Shabbat & Chaggim ❖ **199**

✢ Roll in crumb mixture on both sides and let stand 10 minutes.
✢ Fry chicken pieces in oil until brown on both sides. Chicken will not necessarily be cooked through.
✢ Place pieces on cookie sheet lined with foil and bake for 20 to 25 minutes.
✢ Optional: To serve with orange sauce, use one jar orange marmalade, cooked in small saucepan over medium heat for about 10 minutes to reduce, stirring frequently.

Broccoli-Spinach Casserole

Makes: 12 to 16 servings
Source: Mom

Ingredients

* 2 10-ounce packages frozen chopped broccoli
* 2 10-ounce packages frozen chopped spinach
* 2 sticks margarine (1 cup)
* 4 medium, finely chopped onions
* 2 minced cloves garlic (or 1 teaspoon from jar)
* 1 cup chicken soup (or *pareve* stock)
* 4 tablespoons potato starch
* 4 eggs, beaten
* 1 cup *matzo* meal
* 1/2 teaspoon salt
* 1/4 teaspoon white pepper

Recipe Instructions

* Preheat oven to 350 degrees.
* Cook broccoli and spinach; drain well.
* Melt margarine and sauté garlic and onions in Dutch oven for 10 minutes.
* Remove from heat; stir in chicken soup (or stock) and potato starch, set aside.
* In large bowl, mix vegetables and *matzo* meal, then add soup mixture, salt and pepper; stir well.
* Pour into greased 9 x 13-inch pan and bake for 35 to 40 minutes.

For **Pareve**: *use vegetable or* pareve *stock.*
For **Meat**: *use chicken soup.*

Apple *Matzo* Kugel

Makes: 9 to 12 servings
Source: Mom

Ingredients

* 8 sheets square *matzo*
* 6 eggs
* 1/2 teaspoon salt
* 1/2 cup sugar
* 1/2 cup melted margarine
* 1 pound grated fresh Granny Smith apples with skin (2 to 3 large apples)
* 2-1/2 teaspoons cinnamon

Recipe Instructions

* Preheat oven to 375 degrees.
* Break *matzo* and soak in cold water until soft.
* Drain in colander. Do not squeeze the *matzo*.
* In large bowl, beat eggs well; add salt, sugar, melted margarine, and cinnamon; mix well.
* Add *matzo*; stir in apples.
* Spray 9 x 13-inch glass pan with cooking spray, pour mixture into pan and bake about 30 minutes, until lightly browned.

Apple, Blueberry, and Cherry Cobbler

Makes: 16 to 20 servings
Source: Mom

Ingredients

Topping:
* 1-1/2 cup *matzo* meal
* 3/4 cup potato starch
* 3/4 cup packed brown sugar
* 1/2 teaspoon salt
* 1/4 teaspoon cinnamon
* 3/4 cup chilled margarine cut into small pieces (put in freezer 15 minutes before cutting)
* 3 tablespoon fresh orange juice

Filling:
* 2-1/2 pounds McIntosh apples, sliced, not peeled
* 16 ounces frozen blueberries
* 1 cup sugar
* 8-ounce can sour, pitted cherries, drained
* 1/2 cup fresh orange juice
* 3 tablespoons potato starch
* 1 teaspoon cinnamon
* Cooking spray

Recipe Instructions

* Preheat oven to 350 degrees.

Prepare topping:
* Mix *matzo* meal, starch, brown sugar, salt, and cinnamon together.
* Put into food processor fitted with pastry blade.
* Cut margarine into small pieces and add to ingredients.
* In bowl, pulse blade until mixed into a coarse meal; add three tablespoons orange juice and mix until moist.

Prepare filling:
* Combine apples and next six ingredients; mix gently.

Prepare dish:
* Spray 9 x 13-inch glass pan with cooking spray.
* Press two and a quarter cups topping into bottom of pan.
* Spoon in filling and evenly top fruit with remaining *matzo* mixture.
* Bake for one hour, 10 minutes, or until filling is bubbly and crust is lightly browned.
* Let stand for 10 minutes before serving.
* Can be served warm or chilled in refrigerator and served cold.

Pesach Fudgies

Makes: 20 pieces
Source: Mom

Ingredients

- 4 eggs
- 2 cups sugar
- 1 cup margarine (2 sticks), melted
- 1/2 teaspoon salt
- 6 tablespoons *matzo* cake meal
- 1 cup cocoa
- 1 12-ounce bag chocolate chips

Recipe Instructions

- Preheat oven to 350 degrees.
- Beat eggs until blended; gradually add sugar and beat until light and fluffy.
- Add melted margarine and mix well.
- Sift dry ingredients together and add to egg mixture, stirring until well mixed.
- Stir in chocolate chips.
- Pour into greased 9 x 13-inch glass pan and bake for 20 minutes, not longer.
- Cool completely and cut into squares.

Passover Brownies

Makes: 20 pieces
Source: Mom

Ingredients

- 12 ounces semi-sweet chocolate chips
- 1-1/2 cups margarine (3 sticks)
- 3 cups sugar
- 6 eggs
- 3 teaspoons vanilla extract
- 1 -1/2 cups *matzo* cake meal
- 3/4 teaspoon salt

Recipe Instructions

- Preheat oven to 350 degrees.
- Combine chocolate chips and margarine in small pan, and melt over very low heat; set aside to cool.
- Beat eggs well with electric mixer for five minutes; add sugar and vanilla and mix well.
- Add salt and stir chocolate mixture into eggs by hand.
- Stir in *matzo* cake meal until blended.
- Pour into 9 x 13-inch pan and bake for 30 to 35 minutes, until center is cracked.
- Cool in pan on rack and cut after cool.

Shavuot
The Gift of the Torah

You can find these great recipes in this cookbook that are terrific for *Shavuot*!

❖ Meatless Lasagna
❖ Traditional Thin Crust Pizza
❖ Orange Noodle Pudding
(Pizza & Pasta)

❖ Sweet Potato Casserole
❖ Scalloped Corn Casserole
(Vegetables)

❖ French Onion Soup
❖ Leek, Carrot & Potato Soup
(Soups)

❖ Artichoke Spread
(Salads & Dips)

❖ Cookie Cheesecake
❖ Milk Chocolate Peanut Butter Diamonds
❖ Oma's Crescent Moon Cookies
(Desserts)

See additional Shavuot *recipes on the following pages*

Shavuot provides the greatest revelation of Light of the entire Jewish year. *Shavuot* is the final frontier, the fiftieth gate to open since the intial counting of the *Omer* began on the second night of *Pesach*. It is the pinnacle, the *Keter* (crown), the marriage of *HaShem* to his chosen people, and it commemorates the greatest gift ever given: The Holy Torah.

If we have done our spiritual work correctly, we have just utilized the last 50 days to elevate our *Neshama* and to create a new vessel with which to capture all that is bestowed upon us at this time. We once again commit ourselves in this eternal marriage of the Jewish people with the *Shechina*, G-d's holy presence in this world. On *Erev Shavuot* it is customary, especially for men, to spend the entire night studying *Torah*, *Zohar*, *Tehillim*, works of the *tzadikim*, and more. Sleep is put aside as whoever stays awake and studies *Torah* intensely the entire night is guaranteed by *HaShem* to live until the coming *Rosh Hashanah (Mishnah Berurah 494:1)*. *Shavuot* is a time to experience great awe for *HaShem* as we imagine the tremendous level of *kedusha* (holiness) that must have existed among the Jewish people to merit such a gift from our Creator.

Ashkenazim and Sepharadim have slightly different customs when it comes to preparing meals for the holiday of *Shavuot*. Ashkenazim traditionally eat dairy foods for all meals during this holiday, while Sepharadim will eat meat meals for dinners and dairy meals for mornings and afternoons. Regardless, it is one of the only holidays of the year where preparing dairy dishes is customary. Many families have one or two special dairy recipes that only get attention this one time of the year and everyone looks forward to. Why dairy? Traditionally it is because before Har Sinai we did not know the laws of Kashrut. However, another posit is that dairy is typically white directly related with the branch on the *Etz HaChaim* (Tree of Life) that corrsponds with *chesed*, kindness. On *Shavuot*, *HaShem* reveals his great love and *chesed* (kindness) for the Jewish people through the gift of the *Torah*, the most complex and intricate system of codes that exists on earth. Enjoy this most precious holiday!

Cheese Bourekas

Makes: 12 servings
Source: G.C. Benezra

Ingredients

- 2 eggs
- 2 cups shredded mozzarella cheese
- 1 teaspoon dried parsley
- 1 pinch garlic powder
- 1 pinch onion powder
- 1 pinch salt
- 1 pinch black pepper
- 1 17.5-ounce package frozen puff pastry
- 2 teaspoons water
- 2 tablespoons sesame seeds

Recipe Instructions

- Preheat oven to 350 degrees.
- Grease baking sheet.
- Beat one egg in medium bowl and mix in cheese; season with parsley, garlic powder, onion powder, salt, and pepper.
- On lightly floured surface, cut each sheet of puff pastry into six equal shares for 12 squares total.
- Beat remaining egg with water in small bowl, brush edges of each square lightly with egg wash.
- Place a heaping tablespoon of the cheese mixture in center of each square. Fold pastry over the filling and seal edges with a fork.
- Transfer to the prepared baking sheet, and brush with remaining egg wash. Sprinkle with sesame seeds.
- Bake for 30 minutes or until golden brown; serve immediately.

Mushroom and Cheese Blintzes

Makes: 12 blintzes
Source: From the Chabad.org website

Ingredients

Batter:
- 4 eggs
- 1/2 cup milk
- 1/2 cup water
- 1 cup flour
- 1/4 cup sugar
- 1 package vanilla sugar
- Pinch of salt
- 1 tablespoon oil

Filling:
- 3 tablespoons margarine
- 1 large onion, diced
- 2 cloves garlic, minced
- 2 pounds mushrooms, sliced
- 1/4 cup diced green pepper, optional (can also use some jalapeño pepper for a spicier taste)
- 3 tablespoons flour
- 1 cup milk
- 1/2 teaspoon salt

Continued...

Cheese Bourekas

- 1/8 teaspoon pepper
- 1/2 teaspoon basil
- 1 pound mozzarella or Monterey Jack cheese, grated

Use 7-inch skillet and 10-inch skillet

Recipe Instructions

To prepare batter:
- In a large mixer bowl, combine eggs, milk and water; blend well. Gradually add flour, then both sugars, salt, and oil. Beat well, until there are no lumps in the batter.

To prepare filling:
- Melt margarine in a 10-inch skillet and sauté onion, garlic, mushrooms, and pepper (if used) for 10 to 15 minutes.
- Add flour and stir. Slowly add milk while stirring; add salt, pepper, and basil.
- Cook, stirring over low heat, until mixture thickens; stir in cheese.
- Once thick, set aside.

To assemble crêpes:
- Apply a thin coat of oil to seven inch skillet and place over medium heat, until hot, but not smoking.
- Ladle approximately one-third cup of batter into the skillet; tilt pan to swirl the batter so it covers the bottom of the skillet.
- Fry on one side until small air bubbles form and top is set; bottom should be golden brown.
- When done, carefully loosen edges of crêpe and slip out of skillet onto plate.
- Repeat above procedure until all batter is used; grease skillet as needed.
- Turn each crêpe so that golden-brown side is up. Place three tablespoons of filling on one edge in a two and a half-inch long by one-inch wide mound; roll once to cover filling.
- Fold the sides into the center and continue rolling until completely closed.
- Heat two tablespoons of oil in the skillet and place each filled crêpe seam side down in the skillet. Fry two minutes on each side, turning once.
- Serve warm.

Yahrzeit/Hilulah
Another beautiful time to prepare a special meal

A *yahrzeit*, or *hilulah*, is the anniversary of a person's death. Spiritually speaking, the date of a person's death is as important as his birth. Death is viewed as the time when a person is able to "return home" to the source, when the soul reunites with the Creator.

Traditionally, the death anniversary of a loved one is celebrated through the lighting of a candle in memory of his or her life. However, in some communities, it is also traditional to create a special meal in his or her memory on the death anniversary. People can come to eat, listen to stories about that person, as well as hear words of *Torah*.

Another custom is to celebrate the *yahrzeit* of *tzadikim*, righteous people who lived long ago. The soul of a righteous person is said to leave an opening in the cosmos on the day of his or her departing, and by recognizing the event through the lighting of a candle, eating of a special meal in his or her memory, and studying about the person and his or her contributions, we are able to connect directly to the power that this soul brought into our world. Through the Internet, it is easy to learn about *tzadikim* and the dates of their *yahrzeit*.

To create a special *yahrzeit* meal:
It is truly up to the one hosting the celebration to determine the type of meal it will be. Traditionally, the meal will be a meat meal; however, there are no laws requiring this. In order to make *HaMotzie*, there will need to be enough *challah*, or bread of some kind, for everyone to partake. There is no *Kiddush* at this meal unless it falls on *Shabbat* or a Holiday where *Kiddush* is recited. *Zichrono L'vracha,* may his or her memory be for a blessing.

Shabbat & Chaggim ❋ **209**

Glossary of Terms

Ashkenazim: Jews of Central and Eastern Europe and their descendants.

bitachon: "certainty", as in complete belief and trust.

bracha/brachot: blessing/blessings.

chag/chaggim: holiday/holidays.

chametz: leavened product, forbidden on *Pesach*.

gemara: one of the early records of the oral *Torah*, offering explanations on the *Mishna*; a part of the *Talmud* which are texts used for the study and creation of Jewish law and philosophy.

halacha/halachot: Jewish law/Jewish laws.

HaMotzie: the blessing recited over bread before a meal.

HaShem: Jewish name for G-d.

Kabbalah: Ancient mystical/spiritual study of Judaism, considered to reveal the hidden secrets of the *Torah*; the *Zohar* is one of the primay texts of *Kabbalah*; however, there are several others, as well.

Kiddush: prayer over wine or grape juice.

Mashiach: The Messiah who is destined to bring peace to our world.

middah/middot: personal character trait/traits.

mishloach manot: gift baskets shared on the holiday of *Purim* that traditionally include at least two different foods (ready to be blessed and eaten immediately upon receipt), such as cookies, sweets, nuts, fruits, etc. and possibly a small drink, usually a small bottle of juice.

mitzvah: an act commanded to Jews by *HaShem* either to do, or not do, something. Typically affiliated with good deeds and acts of *chesed*, kindness, to others.

Mussar: the spiritual study in Judaism that promotes the reflection on and refining of one's character.

Neshama: one of the highest levels of a Jewish soul (a term of endearment, plural: *neshamot*).

***Rav*/Rabbi**: a Jewish spiritual mentor, teacher, guide, and authority.

Sepharadim: Jews of Spain and Portugal and their descendants.

Shabbat: the seventh day of the week, from sundown Friday until approximately one hour past sundown on Saturday.

shomer *Shabbat*: "*shomer*" translates as "guardian," someone who is *shomer Shabbat* is someone who "guards the *Shabbat*" by observing the laws revolving around *Shabbat* and its holiness.

siddur: Jewish prayer book.

tikkune: correction or repair a soul must make in order to grow spiritually in this lifetime.

Torah: Also called "The Five Books of Moses," given to the Jewish people from *HaShem* as a beacon of Light and a guidance system for living a Jewish life.

t'shuva: the act of taking upon one's self the laws and *mitzvot*, the improvement of one's self through observances of *halachot*, *chaggim*, *Shabbat*, etc.

tzadik: a person, usually a *Rav* or scholar, that is thought to be an exceptionally spiritual and wise person, someone with tremendous connection to *HaShem*.

tzedaka: traditionally defined as "charity," stemming from the root word "*tzadik*" or "righteous one".

About the Author

On the professional side...

Mia is a clinically licensed psychotherapist with a private practice in Los Angeles, California. In addition to her ten-plus years of experience as a therapist, she has over 20 years of expertise in the worlds of education, non-profit organizations, and public speaking. She is also a professional writer who recently released, *"Insiders Secrets: How to Choose an Exceptional Therapist (and How to Avoid the Bad Ones)"* available for free download on her website. Mia is the Founder and Director of the Channel 4 Change Institute, an educational organization dedicated to promoting the strengthening of women and the uplifting of men and women alike.

On the personal side...

Mia and Shaul married at the start of April 2008, following a six-week courtship. In addition to three beautiful children from her first marriage and four wonderful children from his first marriage, Mia and Shaul also have two little ones together. After a not-so-brief bout of culture shock, Mia began to familiarize herself in the kitchen with the foods her husband adores. She also convinced her husband to periodically trade Moroccan fish for gefilte fish, and slowly her experiences in the kitchen led to this book. Today, the entire family enjoys terrific meals from both the Ashkenazi and Sepharadi traditions.

To contact Mia...

Mia would love to hear from you! Learn more about her and her work at:
www.miaadlerozair.com

Resources

www.MyJewishLearning.com

www.Chabad.org

www.Hillel.org

www.MussarInstitute.org

www.Aish.com

Binah Magazine

www.OUKosher.org

www.LaurenGroveman.com

www.FoodNetwork.com

www.GourmetKosherCooking.com

www.Epicurious.com

www.CookingLight.com

www.JoyOfKosher.com

www.ChefLaurasKosher.com

Index

INDEX
Key for Index:
D=Dairy
KP=Kosher for *Pesach*
M=Meat
P=Parve

Appetizers
- Chicken Wings Mandarin (M), 80
- Chopped Liver (KP, M), 50
- Cocktail Hotdogs (KP, M), 50

Challah
- *Challah* by Food Processor (P), 41
- *Challah* by Hand (P), 39
- Freezing *Challah* Dough, 45
- *Hafrashat Challah*, 37
- Michal's Water *Challah* (P), 43
- *Mitzvah* of *Challah*, 37
  - Pull-apart *Challah*, 45
  - Round *Challah*, 45

Desserts
- Apple, Blueberry, and Cherry Cobbler (KP, P), 202
- Apple Crisp (D, P), 164
- Apple *Matzo* Kugel (KP, P), 201
- Baklava (D, P), 156
- Banana Cake (P), 163
- Brownies, Best Pareve (P), 152
- Brownies, Passover (KP, P), 203

- Cheesecake, Adler Family (D), 161
- Cheesecake, Cookie (D), 148
- Chocolate Covered Dates (P), 166
- Chocolate Peanut Butter Diamonds (D, P), 168
- Fudgies, *Pesach* (KP, P), 203
- Halava, Sesame (P), 159
- *Hamantashen* (P), 190
- Ice Cream, Pareve (KP, P), 167
- Luscious Lemon Squares (P), 155
- Oma's Crescent Moon Cookies (D), 151
- Pumpkin Bread (P), 163
- *Sufganiyot* (D, P), 186
- Taffy Apples (KP, P), 167
- Toffee Squares (P), 158
- Turtle Bars (D, P), 162

Doughs
- Basic Pizza Dough (P), 46
- Popover Rolls (KP, P), 199
- Pretzels, Soft (P), 46
- *Sufganiyot* (D, P), 186

Fish
- Gefilte Fish (KP, P), 94
- Moroccan Fish (KP, P), 97
- Salmon Salad (P), 98
- Simple Salmon (KP, P), 93
- Tuna Salad (P), 98

Glossary of Terms, 210

Kashrut, 27, 197

Meat Dishes
- Bambia (KP, M), 68

- Beauty Roast (KP, M), 56
- Boeuf Bourguignon (M), 75
- Brisket, Honey (KP, M), 55
- Brisket, Mia's Mustard Braised (KP, M), 71
- Brisket, Onions (KP, M), 70
- Brisket, Simple (KP, M), 53
- Chili Con Carne (M), 58
- Cholent, *Shabbat (Hamin)*, (M), 54
- Five-Star Minute Steak (KP, M), 67
- Lauren's Sloppy Joes (KP, M), 73
- Meat Spaghetti Sauce, Oma's (KP, M), 62
- Meatballs, Iraqi with Green Peas (M), 61
- Meatballs, Sweet and Sour (KP, M), 57
- Meatloaf, Ma Catapan's (M), 58
- Rouladen, Oma's (M), 65

Mussar, 25

Neshama, 23

Pizza & Pasta
- Lasagna, Meatless (D), 138
- Noodle Pudding, Orange (D), 144
- Noodles and Rice, Baked (D, M, P), 143
- Pizza, Traditional Thin-Crust (D), 141

Poultry
- Chicken, Almond (KP, M), 199
- Chicken, Forty Cloves Garlic (KP, M), 81
- Chicken, Honey Mustard (KP, M), 84
- Chicken, Saphi's (KP, M), 84
- Chicken, Sepharadi (KP, M), 87
- Chicken, Stir Fry (KP, M), 83
- Chicken, Whole Baked on Kosher Salt (KP, M), 86

- Chicken Wings Mandarin, 80
- *Tabit* (Sepharadi Chicken and Rice) (M), 88

Salads & Dips
- Artichoke Spread (D, KP), 135
- Bean Salad, Three (P), 127
- Corn Salad, Simple (P), 130
- Cucumbers, Sweet and Sour (KP, P), 127
- Egg Salad, Simple (KP, P), 129
- Egg Salad, Spicy (KP, P), 129
- Guacamole, Simple (KP, P), 132
- Hummus (P), 135
- Kamoosh (KP, P, D), 132
- Matbucha (KP, P), 130
- Oriental Salad, Terrific (P), 126
- Potato Salad, Summer (KP, P), 131
- Salmon Salad (P), 98
- Tuna Salad (P), 98

***Shabbat* & *Chaggim*, Recipes**

Chanukah, 185
- Potato Latkes (P), 185
- *Sufganiyot* (D, P), 186

Pesach, 195
- Apple, Blueberry, and Cherry Cobbler (KP, P), 202
- Apple *Matzo* Kugel (KP, P), 201
- Broccoli-Spinach Casserole (KP, P, M), 201
- Brownies, Passover (KP, P), 203
- *Charoset*, Ashkenazi Style (KP, P), 198
- *Charoset*, Sepharadi Style (KP, P), 198
- Chicken, Almond (KP, M), 199
- Fudgies (KP, P), 203
- Rolls, Popover (KP, P), 199

Purim, 184
- *Hamantaschen* (P), 190

***Shabbat* & *Chaggim*, Traditions and Practices**
- *Chanukah*, 185
- *Pesach*, 195
  - *Kashrut* and, 197
  - *Seder*, 195
- *Purim*, 190
- *Rosh Hashanah*, 178
  - *Seder*, 178
- *Shabbat*, 175
  - Preparing for, 175
  - Setting a table, 175
- *Shavuot*, 204
- *Sukkot*, 183
  - Items needed, 183
  - *Mitzvah* of Sitting in *Sukkah*, 183
- *Tishrei*, Month of, 177
- *Tu B'Shvat*, 189
  - *Seder*, 189
- *Yahrzeit/Hilulah*, 209
- *Yom Kippur*, 181

Shavuot, 204
- Cheese Bourekas (D), 206
- Mushroom and Cheese Blintzes (D), 206

Soups
- Asian Shiitake Mushroom Soup (M, P), 116
- Chicken Soup to Heal Your Soul (M, KP), 122
- French Onion Soup (D, P, KP), 114
- Leek, Carrot, and Potato Soup (D, M, P, KP), 117
- *Matzo* Ball Soup, Easy (M, P, KP), 120
- Vegetable Soup (D, P, KP), 119

Index ❋ **219**

Resources, 214

Vegetables
- Broccoli-Spinach Casserole (KP, P, M), 201
- Carrots, Glazed (P, KP), 111
- Corn Casserole, Scalloped (P, D), 105
- Garlic, Roasted (KP, P), 108
- Onions, Baked (D, P, KP), 111
- Potato Latkes (P), 185
- Red Cabbage, Oma's (KP, M), 102
- Red Potatoes, Roasted (KP, P), 108
- Sweet Potato, Baked (KP, P), 104
- Sweet Potato Casserole (D, P, KP), 107